Jane:

Best Wishes

Bill Kelly

FEEDING CHAMPIONS

FEEDING

THE STORY OF
Bil•Jac
THE LIFE AND PASSION
OF BILL KELLY

CHAMPIONS

HOLLY STRAWBRIDGE

Bil•Jac
publications

Published by Bil-Jac Publications
3337 Medina Road, Medina, OH, 44256
www.biljac.com

Distributed by Greenleaf Book Group LLC

For ordering information or special discounts for bulk purchases, please contact Greenleaf Book Group LLC at PO Box 91869, Austin, TX 78709, 512.891.6100.

Design and composition by Greenleaf Book Group LLC
Cover design by Greenleaf Book Group LLC
Photo of Virgil on front cover (top left) and interior was taken by Kurtis Photography in 2000
Photo of Virgil on back cover and interior was taken by Kurtis Photography in 2000
Photo of White Eagle's Celestial Sky on front cover (top right) and interior was taken by Kurtis Photography in 2009
Photo of Spencer on back cover and interior was taken by Kurtis Photography in 2007
Photo of Bill on front cover and interior in front of truck is from the Bil-Jac archive
Photo of patent certificate on front cover and interior is from the Bil-Jac archive
Photo of Kissamee Blackthor Jax on back cover and interior was taken by Debra Freidus, DVM
Photos of Petfood Industry magazine covers in book interior are courtesy of WATT

Publisher's Cataloging-in-Publication Data (Prepared by The Donohue Group, Inc.)

Strawbridge, Holly.
    Feeding champions : the story of Bil-Jac : the life and passion of Bill Kelly / Holly Strawbridge. -- 1st ed.

    p. : ill. ; cm.

    ISBN: 978-0-9824146-0-6

1. Bil-Jac Foods (Firm)--History. 2. Kelly, Bill (William Henry), 1918- 3. Pet food industry--Ohio--History. I. Title.

HD9340.U554 B55 2009
338.7/66466/09771   2009925205

Part of the Tree Neutral™ program, which offsets the number of trees consumed in the production and printing of this book by taking proactive steps, such as planting trees in direct proportion to the number of trees used: www.treeneutral.com

TreeNeutral™

Printed in Canada on acid-free paper

10 11 12 13 14   10 9 8 7 6 5 4 3 2 1

First Edition

In memory of Grinch,
my first Bil-Jac dog,
and for Justine,
who loves it now.

Table of CONTENTS

PREFACE

I have led a great life—a blessed life—and have enjoyed every day in the dog food business. That's why I still go to the office often in my early nineties.

I have always enjoyed animals. Bil-Jac customers are devoted to their pets, and it gives me a good feeling that I can make a super-premium food that helps their pets live long and healthy lives.

There were many challenges along the way, and also many joys. My greatest accomplishment was seeing my three sons enter the family business. They get along with each other, ask for my opinion, and still listen to what I have to say. How lucky can a man be?

I could not have made Bil-Jac a success without my wife. For more than sixty-four years she has been my biggest supporter. I am grateful that she had faith in my vision and stuck by me every step of the way. This book was written for her.

Bill Kelly

Ruth and Bill Kelly, 2004

INTRODUCTION

This is the story of Bil-Jac and its founder, Bill Kelly, a man of uncompromising integrity who has devoted his life to creating the most nutritious dog food possible. Through research and hard work, Bill combined his passion for canine nutrition with an unconventional processing style to create a winning product sold primarily by word of mouth. In the process, Bil-Jac became a thriving family-owned business and a serious competitor in an industry ruled by corporate giants. In the eyes of the Kellys, the real winners are the dogs—the thousands of champions and millions of beloved family pets that have been raised on fresh-tasting, healthy Bil-Jac.

Chapter 1

FEEDING FOXES

Bill Kelly threw on his coat, pulled on warm boots, opened the back door of his family's farmhouse, and stepped into the night. The snow squeaked and crunched under his feet as he crossed the yard toward the barn. Overhead, millions of stars glittered in the brittle blackness of a freezing Ohio night. He opened the door to the dark, dry building, switched on the light, and headed directly for the grinders and mixers. Outside, 220 breeding pairs of silver foxes waited patiently in their pens for breakfast, their fur coats insulating them against the bitter cold. Like he did every morning before school, Bill mixed the fox food, arising in the wee hours before dawn to grind meat for protein and combine it with cereal and vitamins. The recipe, which the Kellys had refined over time, made the animals' coats thick and lush.

Bill didn't mind the chores or getting up in the middle of the night to help his father and their

Bill Kelly with a fox pup

hired hands, Les and Andy Haight. The Kellys were no strangers to hard work. Bill's grandmother Bridget Monohan had emigrated from Ireland to New York City in 1856 at age ten. In only a few years, she was supplying steamships, cruise ships, and hotels from her own produce company on the Lower East Side. It was a remarkable feat for a young, single woman.

Bridget met and married James Kelly, who ran a livery stable near Central Park. Like other Irish eager to escape the potato famine, James had come to the United States seeking a better life. In those days the primary form of transportation was horse and buggy, and there were many stables in New York City. James's stable was thriving. His pride and joy was a white carriage pulled by six white horses, which was immensely popular for weddings.

Irish immigrant Bridget Monohan started a provisioning company in New York City while she was in her teens. Her can-do spirit was passed down to her grandson Bill, who pioneered the first fresh, meat-based dog food in the United States.

James and Bridget had one child, William. William was in college when his father died. The craze for horseless carriages had already hit New York, and William saw the handwriting on the wall. He decided to sell his horses and carriage to a customer in Chicago, where automobiles had yet to make their mark.

On his return to New York by train, William decided to visit a college friend living in Madison, Ohio. The train didn't stop in Madison, but William convinced the conductor to slow down so he could jump off. Unfortunately, he fell down a trestle, breaking his back. At the hospital, he was nursed back to health by an angel named Grace. He thanked her by marrying her.

William divested his livery stable for an excellent price and took a job selling gaslight bulbs in northern New York State. A few years later, he heard about a silver fox breeding farm in Thompson, Ohio, that had gone bankrupt from poor management. With the earnings from the sale, the young couple bought the farm in search of adventure. When the Kellys left New York to start their new life in Ohio, Genevieve (Gene) was ten and William Jr. (Bill) was four. Jack was born in Ohio three years later.

Silver fox are not found in the wild; they occur as genetic mutations of the red fox. Six years after the Kellys began breeding silver fox, another mutant gene appeared, creating a highly valuable color they trademarked as Iridium Platinum.

Young Bill loved working with the animals and was intrigued by how quickly the effects of good nutrition could be seen in their fur. The fox pelts were sold through an auction company in New York, and William took Bill out of school every February for two weeks to help grade the pelts. The experience taught him how to judge the quality of a coat in seconds. "You could attribute a lot of differences in quality to the food the foxes ate," he says.

By the time he reached his midteens, Bill had become enamored with proteins and their amino acids and decided to make animal nutrition his life's work. After graduating from Thompson High School in 1936, he headed to Hiram College to study biology, biochemistry, and nutrition.

Bill loved his classes and was an eager student, but his absence from the fox farm was becoming a great hardship. The new manager who had been hired did not prove to be capable, and that year the foxes produced only 161 of 550 expected pups, providing the Kellys with little income. Bill dropped out of college, intending to return after a semester's absence, but when it became clear that the farm was too much for his parents to manage without him, he stayed on.

Under Bill's guidance, the fox business once again flourished. The combination of superior nourishment and the striking platinum color had produced a valuable fur that was in great demand. Its success enabled the Kellys to buy a larger farm in Medina and double the number of foxes they owned. They also began breeding mink. Business boomed.

Then World War II intervened, and everything changed.

Chapter 2

THE WAR YEARS

In 1942, the United States Armed Services promised farm families they could keep one draft-age child at home, but somehow all three Kelly children ended up serving their country. Gene's nursing skills were put to use in England, where she ran a rest and recuperation home for war-weary American servicemen. Jack became a transportation specialist in the U.S. Army and drove trucks in France. Bill was drafted into the Army in June of 1944.

Bill worked hard to prepare the farm for his departure. Although the two farmhands, Les and Andy Haight, were good workers and kind people, Bill's time at college had made it clear that in his absence, the physical chores involved in running the enormous operation would be a burden to his father, who continued to suffer pain in his back and legs from his train accident. Bill thought that 5- by 15-foot raised pens would be easier for his father to tend and set about building sixty of them. The morning he shipped off to Indiana's Fort Benjamin Harrison for Army induction, Bill arose at 4:00 a.m. and finished the last pen.

• •

New recruits at "Fort Ben" were assigned duties in the kitchen or on the grounds. Bill learned the base was home to a large kennel of German Shepherds being trained to sniff out bombs, and he requested permission from the lieutenant colonel in charge to visit the dogs. Bill was shocked by the conditions he found: The dogs looked ragged and sickly, and the kennel was filthy.

Ch. Loujon Backroad Adventure ("Venture") is the top-winning English Toy Spaniel in the history of the breed—and a Bil-Jac dog. In 2007, he won Best of Breed at Westminster Kennel Club Dog Show and at Crufts in England. Photo by Paul Payne.

THE MAKING OF A CHAMPION...

The quiet buzz of anticipation filled Madison Square Garden on opening morning of the 2007 Westminster Kennel Club Dog Show, the oldest and most prestigious dog show in the world. Hundreds of dog owners, professional handlers, and dog lovers chatted nervously while waiting for their favorite breeds to appear in the ring. On the floor, esteemed judges presided over eight rings of perfectly groomed dogs, which were alternately posing and trotting at the urging of their handlers. More than 2,600 dogs of 165 breeds had earned the right to compete by accumulating enough wins at qualifying shows to be called champions. Now it was time for serious business—awarding Best-of-Breed honors to the best of the best. In the Olympics of dogdom, this is the first step to the coveted Best of Group and Best in Show, and every breeder has both eyes on this prize.

At 11:15 a.m., judge Leonard S. Reppond entered Ring 7 and called for the English Toy Spaniels, B&PC (Blenheim and Prince Charles). The red-and-white and tricolored bundles bounced into view and perkily strutted their stuff, their tails waving like flags and their long, silky fur streaming behind them. The judge evaluated them carefully with experienced eyes, assessing their build, condition, and grooming, and looking for that indefinable quality that "fills the eye."

With knowing hands, the tuxedo-clad judge felt their bones and muscles, stroked their glossy coats, and checked their teeth and eyes before watching them wiggle their way across the carpet. Then without further ado, he pointed his finger at Ch. Loujon Backroad Adventure ("Venture"), a six-year-old with an irresistible smile and award-winning charm, naming him Best of Breed. Only a few months later, Venture went on to win Best of Breed at Crufts in Birmingham, England, the world's largest dog show with more than 24,600 entries. With this medallion added to his accomplishments, Venture became the top-winning English Toy Spaniel in the history of the breed.

Like so many other champions, Venture is a Bil-Jac dog. For more than sixty years, the Kelly family of Medina, Ohio, has manufactured a frozen dog food that produces a thick, soft coat, superior muscle tone, and excellent overall health. Bil-Jac dogs radiate health and happiness, and wrack up so many championships that people have lost count. It's no surprise the food has attained a nearly cultlike status among dog professionals and engenders a passion that other dog food companies can only envy.

"Bil-Jac is a fabulous product. I can't say enough good things about it," says Venture's breeder, owner, and handler, Karen Miller of Loujon Kennels in Detroit, Michigan. "I've fed Bil-Jac for over thirty years, and during this time, other dog food companies have come to me and said, 'Buy our product.' But my feeling is that if it ain't broke, don't fix it."

"It shouldn't be this way," he told his superior. "Let me help."

The commander agreed, and Bill called home to request food for the scraggly, undernourished animals. His father immediately sent a truck with fresh meat, cereal, and supplements to mix for the dogs. Bill dug out the runs, replaced the dirt with smooth pebbles for better drainage and sanitation, and added shavings to the bedding area. In no time at all, the dogs were looking and performing far better. The lieutenant colonel was so pleased that he retained Bill for four weeks past the recruits' usual ten-day stay.

For Bill, working with the dogs was heaven. "I told them I'd like to be assigned to the Canine Corps because I enjoyed the dogs so much," he says. The officer in charge agreed it was a splendid idea and offered to put in a word for him. Assignments were classified, however, so the officer would not be told where Bill would be sent for basic training.

Bill was assigned to a base in Utah, and he assumed there was a kennel there. But en route to the new base he was taken off the train in Colorado, where he was commandeered for the Air Corps to be educated not in animal care but in electronics.

Photo by Asbey Photography

9

Bill had no interest in electronics. Nevertheless, he proved to be a quick learner with talent for the field. He was sent first to Illinois, then to Florida for increasingly detailed education. The Air Corps needed a way to improve the ability of bombs dropped from 39,000 feet to hit their targets and was recruiting men to work on equipment that would make adjustments for wind velocity and distance. Bill's team was assigned to develop an oscillating radarscope for bombers. The project was classified, and the engineers were not given any details. Their every move was closely watched.

Bill Kelly and Ruth Willey after their engagement

"We knew something was up, but we had no idea what it was," says Bill. "I lived off the base, and for a year and a quarter, I was followed everywhere I went. One day, my dad called and said, 'Gee, the Secret Service, the FBI—everybody's here checking you out.'"

Finally, the team was transferred to New Mexico, where they tested their invention by dropping two-and-a-half-ton bags of flour from B-29 bombers onto round, room-size targets. "They'd go 'pouf' when they hit. We could see it clearly, even from 39,000 feet. I had the best record hitting the target," says Bill.

Bill enjoyed acting as bombardier, but his talents nearly landed him a dubious place in the history books. He had been assigned to the Manhattan Project. But before Bill's team was called into action, two atomic bombs effectively brought the Japanese to the peace table.

"I would have been assigned to hit Tokyo Harbor," says Bill solemnly. "I'm glad I never had to do it. It bothered me that they dropped the bomb on populations, but I had the opportunity to talk to President Truman two years later and told him I appreciated his guts."

. . . .

In 1940, shortly before the U.S. entered the war, the basketball coach at the high school in nearby Granger, Ohio, enlisted in the service, and Bill, who had always enjoyed sports, took over his job. Among the friends he made at the school was the custodian, Lloyd Simon.

One day the following winter, Lloyd invited Bill to go tobogganing. Lloyd's wife invited her sister, Ruth Willey, to come along. Ruth's sweet personality appealed to Bill, and he asked her out on a date.

"Do you know where he took me? To one of those noisy car races!" says Ruth, still sounding amazed more than sixty years later. "He thought he would impress me, but he didn't," she says, shaking her head.

Despite his unsuccessful choice of dating activities, Bill tried again the following week. This time, the couple went to a rodeo. Ruth didn't care much for that either. "I would've much rather gone to a romantic movie," she says.

Bill got the hint and started taking his new girlfriend on more suitable dates. Their love for each other grew, but the war nearly threw a wrench in the relationship. When Bill was drafted, Ruth decided she didn't

want to be a war bride. Eventually, though, she changed her mind. "I agreed to marry him if I could follow him around the country," she says.

After several months of long-distance dating, Bill took leave in December 1944 and returned to Medina so he and Ruth could become husband and wife. When he arrived home, he found his mother and father in poor health and the farm in sad shape. Grace's eyesight had deteriorated. William's back and legs still caused him a great deal of pain.

Bill Kelly took military leave to marry Ruth Willey on December 6, 1944.

"My parents' health was gone—they had worried so much about us," Bill says.

Times were tough due to the demands of a country at war. Most able-bodied men were in the service or working in defense plants, and help was hard to come by. Les and Andy Haight couldn't handle the farm alone. As a result, William had

starting selling off the foxes and was down to about twenty pairs.

While home on furlough, Bill closed down the fox farm. No one knew how long the war would last, but now, after selling all their foxes, the Kellys had enough money to ride it out securely.

• •

Before the United States became involved in the war, the prevailing attitude was optimistic, and this was reflected in the popularity of fur coats. Silver fox brought more money than any other fur. After the attack on Pearl Harbor, however, people gradually stopped buying luxury goods.

When the war ended in August 1945, Bill and Ruth headed back to Medina as fast as possible in their 1932 Chevy. "It had been a difficult period, and we were so happy to get back home," Ruth remembers.

The young couple settled in an upstairs apartment in the Kelly home and enjoyed their families while considering what to do next. Bill quickly received many job offers in electronics and interviewed with

several companies. He was greatly impressed by the quality of the electrical engineers he met.

"One company had hired seven of the top electronics people in the country and built special labs for them, because they were working on developing the television," he remembers. "At night I would go work with them and learn. 'Call me when you get the first wavelength,' I told them, and they did. It was three o'clock in the morning. I got there and saw the wave on the screen. That was the first television," says Bill.

Although he could have made a good living in electronics, Bill didn't like the thought of being cooped up. "I was an outdoor boy and couldn't see living all my years behind the four walls of a lab," he says.

Bill Kelly on leave from the Army, inspecting his family's fox farm.

The need to make a living was pressing on the young couple, who were down to their last $38 in severance pay, when Bill had a brainstorm. "We had the equipment to make fox food—grinders, mixers, and coolers. I thought it might be a good idea to make dog food," he says, adding that dogs are similar to foxes in that they are both carnivores and need a meat-based diet.

Bill labored on the idea, because his product was going to cost more than dog foods made by grain mills. He didn't know how long it would be before they would make any money—if they made money at all.

Finally, Bill shared his idea with Ruth, who was somewhat perplexed. Her dad had never bought dog food: the family dogs simply ate table scraps. But her reply reflected her faith in her husband's judgment. "If that's what you want to do, go for it," she told him.

MAKING DOG FOOD

Bill thinks it might have been his experience at boot camp that triggered his interest in making dog food. "It proved that our fox food really could do something for dogs, and that I could master the formula," he says.

But his decision more likely arose from a series of events that had prepared him to meet the needs of a market void. Growing up, Bill had been keenly aware that the dogs on his family's fox farm that ate the meat-based fox food had a distinct advantage in health and appearance over his friends' pets that were raised on commercial dog food.

At the time—1946—there were about forty-two companies in the state of Ohio making dog food, primarily from grains. "The food was not high quality at all," says Bill. That's because its protein source was the gluten extracted from the grains. Today, these are known as gluten meals or protein concentrates. Proteins are comprised of twenty-two amino acids, ten of which are essential and must be provided in the dog's diet in a readily digestible form. While gluten meals are

Bill Kelly was determined to offer pet lovers a better dog food. To accomplish his goal, he avidly studied animal nutrition, marketing, and business.

THE CASE OF THE AILING RETRIEVER ....

In the 1970s, Dr. Robert Green was one of five veterinarians in a Tulsa, Oklahoma, practice when a couple came to the clinic requesting an arthritis medication for their Golden Retriever. With disconcerting frankness, they said if they could not find something that would help their dog walk better, they would put it to sleep. Dr. Green agreed to write a prescription on the condition that if the medication did not produce results in short order, they would bring the dog to the clinic for an examination.

The following week, the couple showed up with their chubby Retriever, who was barely able to walk into the exam room. But it was immediately apparent that walking was only one if its problems.

"The dog was not only in pain, it was also clearly in distress. It stunk, and its coat looked greasy and awful," Dr. Green recalls.

While he examined the sick pet and drew blood samples, he asked the owners what dog food they used. Two popular brands of light dog food and treats, they responded. Dr. Green did the math: The dog was getting 1,200 calories a day—an amount low enough to produce weight loss. However, the calories were "junk."

"Light dog foods are high in fiber, which inhibits the absorption of protein, carbohydrates, and nutrients. Some dogs do well on light foods, but this dog was not one of them. He was overweight but starving," says Dr. Green.

Instead of prescribing another medication, Dr. Green suggested the owners substitute one cup of their dog's regular food with one cup of Bil-Jac twice a day.

The following week, the couple returned with their Retriever, who had already lost several pounds and was clearly feeling better. The initial exam had revealed an enlarged prostate, so the dog was neutered and left on a Bil-Jac diet. One month later, it had lost nearly ten pounds and was showing a better coat. By three months, it had achieved its desired weight, was moving freely without pain medication, and no longer smelled.

"Neutering should have caused the dog to gain weight, but this dog was thinner and happier," says Dr. Green, who used to relate the story in talks to veterinary students. While he didn't know scientifically how Bil-Jac could produce such results, he enjoyed telling the students about dogs like this one whose health had been improved by the nutritious food.

"I rarely had a failure on Bil-Jac. It's the best food out there," he says.

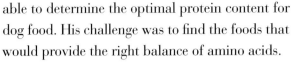

high in protein, they do not contain the proper balance of these essential amino acids and are not readily digestible, making them poor sources of canine nutrition.

"There was a big need for something better," says Bill. He worked hard to come up with a premium dog food made from high-quality protein derived from fresh meat and other fresh ingredients. His first challenge was to find the right formula. "It had to be a different mix than we used for the foxes, because it needed to be compatible with enzymes in the dog's digestive system," he explains.

For advice and direction, he turned to Professor J. Turner, his former science teacher at Hiram College. The two men shared a passion for amino acids. With Turner's guidance, Bill was

The first bag of frozen Bil-Jac, manufactured for sale on January 8, 1947.

able to determine the optimal protein content for dog food. His challenge was to find the foods that would provide the right balance of amino acids.

"Each individual protein is distinctly different from all others. The difference is found in the amount of each amino acid in the protein, the specific sequence of the amino acids in the molecule chain, and the manner in which the molecule chain is folded and connected. These differences determine various properties of proteins, including their nutritive value for metabolic synthesis in a dog. The more closely the pattern of amino acids of a food resembles the pattern of dog proteins, the higher its biologic value to dogs will be," Bill explains.

Because dogs are carnivores, Bill started with 50 percent meat in the form of beef, liver, selected beef by-products, and chicken. The meat was fresh and naturally juicy, so it was not necessary to add water. "Water dilutes the goodness that makes it palatable," says Bill.

The next ingredient he added was wheat that had been cooked completely to convert the complex carbohydrates to simple starches. Dogs need carbohydrates to neutralize protein metabolites and to supply energy. Bill also added fiber in the form of beet pulp ground to the ideal texture to facilitate digestion. This type of fiber works the small intestine gently, aiding in digestion without causing intestinal stress while producing a firmer stool.

Vitamins and minerals were added last. "Although vitamins are required in very small amounts, a lack of any one will result in a specific, predictable deficiency. Our formula was balanced with the proper supplemental vitamins to give dogs optimum nutrition," says Bill.

Supplemental calcium and phosphorus were added for bone health, and trace minerals were added for the biosynthesis of essential nutrients and the utilization of energy and protein. Finally, Bill added cane molasses, a great natural source of B vitamins and iron.

One ingredient he did not add was fat. "The fresh meat had sufficient natural fat to maintain the dogs' health and to improve the eyes, skin, and coat. The natural fat was distributed evenly throughout the food and made it extremely tasty," he says.

Bill worked for months to refine the formula, testing each new batch on the mink, which they had kept when the foxes were sold. With their short digestive tracts, mink are ideal for

nutrition research. Only two-and-a-half hours after consuming a meal, they produce a stool that can be analyzed to determine how well the animal has utilized its food. The ability to obtain quick answers enabled Bill to accomplish in a few months what would have taken years of testing on dogs.

The Kelly family's Collies, Ruth's Cockapoo, and their Miniature Schnauzer also assisted in product development by participating in palatability testing. They loved the food, and their enthusiasm for helping was unbounded. As a result, nothing went to waste.

"We had a small mixer, so the test batches were small," says Bill.

• •

Once Bill was satisfied with the formula for his dog food, he had to find a way to make a fresh food that was neither too wet nor too dry, was easy to serve, looked appealing, and could be reliably reproduced.

"The first batch I made in the mixer came out lumpy," he recalls.

Bill thought a pellet-shaped food might be easiest to handle, but no machine that could

produce such a shape was available. He tried putting the batch through a grinder, but the mixture was too heavy. He had to innovate. He finally ordered a custom grinder with a long choke that would enable him to extrude the meaty mass with minimal pressure. A built-in knife cut the food into pieces. The machine worked beautifully, producing a product that looked like large pieces of hamburger.

To preserve the freshness and nutrients in his dog food, Bill froze it. The food simply needed to be thawed to be served.

By the first week of January 1947, Bill had achieved his goal. William recommended calling the new dog food Bil-Jac, after Bill and his brother Jack, who was a partner in the venture.

But in 1947, there were no guarantees the fledgling venture would succeed. "We used fresh meat, eggs, liver, and chicken, which ended up costing about 50 percent more than what regular dog food cost. I didn't know whether I'd make enough to feed the family or not," Bill says. Fortunately, friends and neighbors in Medina were eager to help. Although Bill had not had any income for a few years, he was able to borrow enough money from a local bank to start the business.

The first batch of Bil-Jac made for sale weighed about three hundred pounds. On the first day, Bill sold six two-pound bags for 25 cents apiece to six neighbors, including Les Haight. Bil-Jac was on its way.

Bil-Jac was the first dog food to be granted a U.S. patent.

With its unique formulation and manufacturing process, Bil-Jac was eligible for a patent. Bill applied, and in 1951 Bil-Jac became the first dog food granted a U.S. patent. Subsequent developments in processing enabled Bill to renew the patent seventeen years later.

• •

Making the product turned out to be the easy part. Sales and distribution were bigger challenges. The Kellys gained customers by going house to house and knocking on doors.

Every morning, Bill arose early to mix the food. He then headed out to make sales calls. Family by family, dog by dog, the business grew. Bill got people to try it with a novel marketing method—free samples. "I told them to place a dish of Bil-Jac alongside a dish of their dog's regular food and see which one their dog chose. Being a fresh product, it was very palatable, and the dogs always chose the Bil-Jac," said Bill.

The two-bowl challenge never failed. The next day, the phone would ring at the Kellys'

with an order, which Bill would make fresh and deliver the following day. Ruth did the bookkeeping at night.

In the 1940s, Northern Ohio was home to a large number of dog breeders, many of whom operated large boarding kennels on the side. Bill would stop by the kennels, explain how Bil-Jac was different from commercial foods, and leave challenge packs with the owners. It didn't take long for dog professionals to see the impact Bil-Jac made on their show dogs as well as on their boarders' dogs. Then a funny thing began to happen.

"The customers would go home, and their dogs would refuse to eat their usual food. They would call the kennel owners, who would explain that the dogs had been fed Bil-Jac. Then the customers would call us and place an order," says Bill.

In 1948, Jack was returning from a delivery run when his truck overturned, breaking his back. Bill's wife and sister took over Jack's routes.

"Gene could drive that old truck—I couldn't—so she drove, and I took the bags of food to the customers' doors," Ruth recalls.

Chapter 4

BUILDING LOYAL CUSTOMERS

Through house-to-house calls and home-made flyers, Bil-Jac grew one customer at a time. "People who wanted the product called us, and we delivered it," says Bill.

Selling directly to veterinarians gave the business a jump start. In the 1940s there were only a handful of veterinarians in Northern Ohio, so they were highly influential with clients. One of the most common complaints among dog owners was that their dogs had loose stools. It was a condition Bil-Jac could cure in no time at all.

"The grain-based foods flushed right through the dogs," said Bill. The vets soon realized what good nutrition could do and readily spread the word about Bil-Jac.

Bill gave veterinarians freezers to ensure that Bil-Jac was properly stored and always available in their offices. "The freezers were the biggest cost of setting up, but they were worth it," he says.

At that time, Ohio was a hotbed of dog professionals. Norbill Kennels, the biggest breeder of Cocker Spaniels in the country, was located in Berea. Silojet Kennels in Medina bred champion Poodles. There were two top breeders of Great Danes in the area, veterinarians Dr. Jim Robertson and Dr. Robert Biddle. In the southern part of the state, the owners of Procter & Gamble ran Hedrington Kennels.

Bil-Jac was ideally situated in the middle of it all. But the competition was not intimidated by this new dog food on the market. Ken-L Biskit, made by the Quaker Oats subsidiary Ken-L Ration, had grown to become the first choice of

SeaWorld animal trainer Joel Slaven with Diego (left) and Floyd (right), two shelter rescues used in SeaWorld's animal shows. Joel uses frozen Bil-Jac instead of treats to train his dogs to perform complicated routines because he finds they love the food enough to work for it day after day. Photo by Andrea LeBlond.

WILL WORK FOR FOOD............

SeaWorld is the country's premier marine theme park, but hundreds of animals and birds also call the entertainment destination home. In fact, all five theme parks owned by Busch Entertainment Corporation—three SeaWorlds and two Busch Gardens—have animal shows run by Joel Slaven, one of the most skilled professional animal trainers in the country. Joel and his staff work one-on-one with the dogs, cats, rats, pigs, birds, and various other critters, teaching them how to perform in a variety of comical and dramatic situations.

All but a handful of exotic animals in these shows were unwanted pets rescued from local animal shelters and Humane Societies. Five or six times a year, Slaven visits these locations looking for animals that are friendly, calm, and responsive to food. If they meet these qualifications, he adopts them and takes them to live, play, and work in ideal accommodations on the theme park grounds.

Slaven and Anheuser-Busch executives work together to create a theme for each show, which is different in every park and changes on a regular basis. In 2007, the animals in SeaWorld Orlando performed in a charming show called "Pets Ahoy." It starred a nine-year-old Rottweiler mix named Tank. Tank was one of the dogs Slaven plucked from an Orlando shelter and fingered for stardom. Big on personality as well as looks, Tank clearly loved to perform, and the audiences adored his shtick.

"If you want to win the heart of your girlfriend, you have to take her on a date," trainer Shannon Dennison would tell Tank before walking off the stage set that resembles a seaside village.

Alone in the spotlight and seemingly without prompting, Tank would trot over to a pay phone, take the receiver off the hook, drop it, and bark his invitation into the receiver. He quickly ran up the stairs to an ATM machine, poked a button, and pulled out a bill. Racing across the boardwalk to a store, he inserted the bill into a slot. A door popped open, and he reached in to retrieve a bouquet of flowers. With the flowers in his mouth, he descended the wooden stairway and hopped into a waiting jeep. A couple of beeps on the horn, and he drove away to pick up his date.

Training dogs to do such complex acts requires a lot of rewards, and all SeaWorld trainers rely solely on Bil-Jac to motivate their dogs.

"They will work very hard for it. In fact, they are happy to work for it," says Slaven, who goes through forty pounds a day of frozen Bil-Jac in Orlando alone. Pieces of the thawed frozen food are used in place of treats because the pieces are easy to handle and crumb-free.

At the end of an average day, the dogs have received dozens of rewards and should not be hungry. Come dinnertime, however, they wolf down a bowl of Bil-Jac with gusto.

"They love it, and that's the bottom line," says Slaven.

But what tastes good is also nutritionally sound, and that's important for animals that spend their lives in the public eye.

"Our animals have beautiful coats and are strong, healthy, and happy, so you know what they are eating is good for them. If we fed them food that was not so good, it would catch up with them sooner or later," says Slaven.

After many years on stage, some of the animals lose their desire to perform. These lucky dogs are usually adopted by one of the trainers and taken home to spend their days snoozing on the sofa. Because the dogs are so healthy, their retirement years can be many.

"Seems our dogs live forever. Some of them started ten years ago at the age of two or three, have been adopted, and the trainers still have them after several years," says Slaven.

breeders, and Bill's primary challenge was to lure those users over to Bil-Jac.

Another competitor, Cincinnati-based Yankee Foods, the maker of Hill's brand dog foods, relied on guilt to motivate sales. Their sales pitch was, "Remember, we took care of you during the War." But as Bil-Jac made inroads, Yankee Foods was gradually pushed out of the Northern Ohio market.

By 1949, the appeal of a fresh frozen product had begun to make a dent in the competitors' revenues. That year, two companies that made dry dog food tried to put Bil-Jac out of business by giving away more food than the Kellys sold. The plan didn't work.

"We just kept plugging away, knowing we had the real McCoy," says Bill.

The family business kept growing as Gene's husband, Ralph Goodwin, joined the company in 1956 to handle a portion of the sales responsibilities. Bil-Jac kept growing its customer base by adding pet product retailers, such as feed mills and pet shops.

Over the succeeding years, Bill's marketing tactics and the reputation of Bil-Jac created such demand for the food that the company began to expand by hiring beyond immediate family. In the early winter of 1957, Medina resident Larry Taft was hauling coal for a local business when his pickup truck slipped off a snowy road. Bill Kelly just happened to be driving on the same road, and he stopped to help pull Taft's truck out of the ditch. The two men were acquainted, and in fact, Taft had visited the Kelly farm on several occasions.

A few days later, it was Bill's turn to get stuck in the snow. This time, Taft helped Bill out. Bill offered him a job delivering Bil-Jac, and he accepted. In addition to delivering orders, Taft picked up products at the stockyards. Ever conscious of picking only the highest quality meats, Bill had obtained greater control by cutting out the middleman.

In no time at all, Taft asked to transition into sales. He was a natural salesman. If he drove by a house and spotted a dog in the yard, he would stop, knock on the door, and offer the owners a challenge pack.

"I loved the job, because of the people I met. If you had dogs, I would talk to you about what the dog food was going to do for them. I would tell you it was going to save you money because you were going to feed much less," says Taft.

Taft was ambitious. He came in every night, called store managers, and made up his own list of clients. He wasn't

afraid to make cold calls to stores, stopping in with samples of Bil-Jac. His route quickly grew. "I picked up new people all the time and kept putting new orders on the truck. When a route got too big, we'd split it," he says.

A "people person" through and through, Taft was fond of all his clients, but his greatest satisfaction came from selling Bil-Jac to veterinarians. "I'd go in and say, 'Here's a sample I want you to feed your own dog,' and the vet would say, 'Ain't gonna work.'

"Well, I'd go back a little later and the vet would say to me, 'You got a delivery truck coming through here anytime soon?'" he recalls with a chuckle. "Once they saw what the food could do, they liked the product. That's because Bil-Jac is not just great—it's the best! You can tell the difference in a Bil-Jac dog over another dog." The best part, says Taft, was that all he had to do was tell the truth.

Taft's delivery route included mink ranchers who bought the original mink food formula from the Kellys. One of the mink farmers fed fresh Kelly mink food to half his stock, and another product to the other half. The benefits of the better food were evident to everyone. "It'd just blow your mind—you could see the difference in

the fur so quick, and there was much less stool on the fresh meat side than on the other side," Taft recalls.

Comparisons were equally effective on dogs, and particularly amazing on runts. Runts are small due to their position in utero: The first dog on the nutrition chain gets the most and grows the largest; the last puppy—the runt—gets cheated. However, it is possible to make up the difference after birth. "I'd tell breeders, 'Give me the runt, the smallest one in the litter, and I'll make him one of the big guys,'" says Taft.

A German Shepherd breeder with a new litter accepted his challenge and fed Bil-Jac to the runt of her litter. "I think she did it as a joke, but that runt grew up to be a champion. He was absolutely beautiful—and you should have seen his coat!" says Taft proudly.

While Bill and Larry made headway in sales, new orders began coming in so fast that there was little time for the men to call on existing clients. In 1959 Bill hired Kay Bowman to handle customer relations. Kay had been working at a brokerage house, but after her third child was born, she wanted to scale back to part-time. Lucille Burton, the office manager at Bil-Jac, knew Kay and thought the Bil-Jac job would be a perfect match.

At that time, the Bil-Jac "corporate offices" were located in the rear of a building that had belonged to a blacksmith. In the storefront, the Kellys had set up a small store that sold hardware, paint, seeds, and other goods for area farmers and homeowners. Kay did double duty by working the cash register, mixing paints, and mopping the floor. Of course, she also called customers to ask whether they needed more Bil-Jac.

By the time Kay's youngest child was in kindergarten, the offices had been moved to the Kelly family homestead on Granger Road, still near Kay's in-laws. This made it very convenient for Kay to keep her eyes on her daughter, who would stay with her grandparents for a few hours after school. At

Mutual respect between the Kellys and their employees— known as "associates"—makes Bil-Jac a wonderful place to work. Many employees spend decades with the company. Of the original staff shown here with Bill Kelly, Kay Bowman (lower left) spent 39 years at Bil-Jac, Lucille Burton (lower right) more than 20 years, and Lenora Codding (upper right) 16 years.

5:00 p.m., Kay would simply swing by, pick up her daughter, and head home.

A few more local residents were hired to work at Bil-Jac, which made their jobs even more enjoyable. "It was a good time, a very good time," Kay remembers. Most of all, she loved working for the Kellys. "They are such nice people—very down-to-earth. We had cows, and sometimes they would get out. Bill would help me get the cows back in. He was just like family," she says.

Bill insisted that every established customer be called on a regular basis to see whether they needed more Bil-Jac. Depending on how much the customers used, they were called weekly or every two weeks. At the end of a day, Kay would submit the orders, which the drivers would use to load their trucks the next morning.

Kay was a huge hit with clients. Five days a week, she made phone calls to local stores, kennels, pet stores, and individual dog owners. She was so disciplined in her calls, in fact, that many clients would get worried if her call came a few minutes late. "Kay, where have you been? You're always on time," they'd say. Then Kay would ask them how they were, and they would get to chatting.

Sometimes customers would cry on the phone. "When I asked them what was the matter, they would tell me their problems. I'd give them sympathy, and I would check on them between calls to see how they were doing," Kay remembers.

When a customer or member of a customer's family got sick, Kay would send a card. When a customer passed away, she would go to the funeral home. "I loved them all. I never met some of them until years later, but by talking with them on the phone, we became like family," she says.

Like all Bil-Jac employees past and present, Kay was sold on the product and eager to provide outstanding service. So when customers ran out of Bil-Jac, Kay would make sure they got the food right away. "The customer always came first," she says.

Chapter 5

THE DOG SHOW CIRCUIT

In the late 1940s, dog shows were popular places to see and be seen. Nowhere in the country were they bigger than in Northern Ohio. Maxwell Riddle of Ravenna, who was instrumental in developing the Ravenna, Chagrin Valley, and Western Reserve Kennel Clubs, was a personal friend of F. Scott Fitzgerald, and his shows drew celebrities and national attention.

Bill figured that such shows would be fertile ground for reaching potential customers. He bought a freezer, filled it with samples, and set up a Bil-Jac booth at every show. At that time, Ken-L Ration sponsored many of the shows, and a representative of Quaker Oats was always present. Bil-Jac gave the competition a run for its money.

"Because our food was a meat-based product, it was an easy sell. I would hand out samples and say, 'Test it against what you're feeding.' But I would also give them information about how it was made, talk about its nutritional value, and tell them that it would put good muscle tone and a good coat of fur on their dogs. Even today, nobody can put a coat on a dog like Bil-Jac can," says Bill.

Through his research, Bill unlocked the secret of why Bil-Jac makes a dog's coat shiny and healthy. It's the result of a survival mechanism developed over countless generations to ensure nutrition goes where it is needed. "When a dog eats, it uses its food to benefit its internal organs, muscles, skin, and coat in that order. That's why

Breeder and handler Jack Patterson has fed Bil-Jac to his dogs for years. More than once, he credits the food for saving the life of a champion.

DOCTORING DOGS . . . .

Any sick dog is a problem, but a sick Saint Bernard is a very big problem indeed.

"We were showing a Saint Bernard—the number two Saint in the United States—when he became lethargic and started losing weight. We doctored with this and that, but nothing worked. Suddenly he went off his food," handler Jack Patterson recalls. "Fortunately, I've used nothing but Bil-Jac for thirty years. We wadded it up into little balls and hand-fed him."

The Pattersons spent weeks trying to get to the root of the dog's troubles. "I can't tell you how many vets we saw. It took a while for him to be diagnosed with

Rocky Mountain spotted fever, which he had gotten from a tick bite. Once he started on antibiotics, he came back quickly, but we had kept him going by hand-feeding him Bil-Jac," says Patterson.

It may be hard for owners of eager eaters to believe, but some breeds are naturally poor eaters, even when they are healthy. Dogs who simply don't like to eat are found in every breed, and hand-feeding is sometimes the only way to keep them alive.

"I showed a Mastiff for three years, and during that time, he never ate a meal. He would sit there, open his mouth, and I'd stuff in the Bil-Jac," Patterson recalls.

Because the Bil-Jac food is easy to handle, it is easier to use than dry food or canned food, and there is less waste. "When you look at my dogs, you see their coats are gorgeous. They stay that way until the day they die," Patterson says.

"I can tell you one thing: If a dog on Bil-Jac is having a digestive problem or a bowel problem, you better start looking for a vet, because it's not the dog food."

dogs that are poorly nourished have skin problems and poor coats," Bill says.

"We discovered that a simple muscle cell lasts about two weeks before it sloughs off and goes back into the bloodstream. Dogs reuse the protein in those cells in time of stress," he explains. "A dog's coat is almost 90 percent protein, and there's no way that a dog could eat that much food, so they tap the reserve from old muscle cells to build their coats. With its ideal nutritional composition, Bil-Jac builds better muscle tone on a dog than any other food, and it shows in the coat."

• •

The Bil-Jac Pet Food Diner at the 1959 Cleveland Dog Show. From left to right, Jack Kelly, two unidentified men, Ralph Goodwin Jr., Ralph Goodwin Sr. (Bill Kelly's brother-in-law), Bob Kelly, Ray Kelly, Rick Goodwin.

Bill worked the dog show circuit for thirty-five years, and although he enjoyed it, the busy schedule took too much time away from developing other markets. It became clear that a dedicated person to work the dog shows was needed. In 1984, Bill hired Dick Becker to represent Bil-Jac at dog shows. Dick and his wife, Phyllis, were well connected at all levels of the dog show world. In addition to breeding and showing Old English Sheepdogs, Dick worked for Ethelynn Harrison, a handler who counted among her clients Mrs.

Geraldine Rockefeller Dodge, founder of the English Cocker Spaniel Club of America. Other breeders and handlers listened to what Dick had to say, because Dick knew dogs: From 1975–79, he handled the number one English Cocker Spaniel in the United States with two different dogs—Ch. Maplelawn Jasper Johns and Ch. Applewyn Angus.

Phyllis Becker was a licensed dog show superintendent, a job she retains to this day. Like other show people, the Beckers spent most of their time on the road, traveling to dog shows across the country in their RV.

With Dick on board, Bil-Jac was represented at all major shows and many smaller shows. The sales force set up the Bil-Jac booth and stocked it, and Dick sold Bil-Jac like crazy.

Several other breeders and handlers became so attached to Bil-Jac that they asked to become dealers. One was Michael Kemp of Houston, who now lives in Pennsylvania. Like Becker, Kemp had tremendous credibility with his peers, and this translated into sales.

"I bought about 40,000 pounds of Bil-Jac every eight to ten weeks. I would get it at the dog shows, and bring it home and put it in a large, walk-in freezer I had built at my kennel. I liked it because the dogs ate it, their condition was good, and they produced good stools. Their bowls were licked clean. The kennel was clean, because they burned up so much of the food that they didn't drop stool all the time. When we traveled with them, their crates were clean," Kemp says.

When Kemp started as a Bil-Jac dealer in Houston, he couldn't keep the food in stock. "All the dog handlers wanted it. They came from all over the area to get it from me because they had

Photo by Chuck and Sandy Tatham.

Registry's Lonesome Dove, shown here winning Best in Show at the 1992 Westminster Kennel Club Show, was the second-highest-winning show dog of all time. A real trooper, "Lacey" was on top of her game every time she entered the ring. Handler Michael Kemp attributed her winning attitude and top form to Bil-Jac.

used as much as they could get at the dog shows. I even had people from California asking me to ship it to them when they found out I carried it," he says.

For dog shows in the Houston area, Kemp would set up a booth with a freezer full of Bil-Jac. The handlers bought it so fast he had to restock every day. "When we got down to the last day, they would order a lot and take off with it when the show was over," he says.

They wanted Bil-Jac because they knew Kemp fed it to his dogs, and his dogs were winners. First he handled a Bichon Frisé named Devon Puff n Stuff, who earned sixty Best in Shows and became the highest-winning Bichon of all time. Her record stood until the late 1980s.

After she retired, Kemp handled a Wire Fox Terrier named Registry's Lonesome Dove ("Lacey"). Lacey not only became the winningest terrier of all time, but she also has the honor of being the second-highest-winning show dog of all time. With a total of 216 Best in Shows, she was almost unbeatable.

Kemp is proud of treating his dogs like athletes. An important part of their conditioning is nutrition—which, Kemp says, is synonymous with Bil-Jac.

"I feed Bil-Jac because I have the greatest confidence in the world in it. When you have dogs that are under stress and can perform show after show like Lacey did, it's remarkable. She never tired, never gave up, never quit. She was on top of her game at all times. She had a great brain and a great heart, but she also was in top shape and felt good, and I attribute this to her dog food," says Kemp. "I won't stop feeding Bil-Jac, because it works for me. Even after I quit handling dogs, I will still use it on my own dogs."

Chapter 6 ....

THE NORWAY YEARS

In December 1949, Bill was at the Cleveland Dog Show when he met a young man named Paul Iams. Paul was originally from Dayton, but after being discharged from the Navy, he went to work for a dog food company in Columbus and was representing their canned food at the show.

The two men discovered they shared a deep interest in animal nutrition. They were also both developing their own dog food formulas. But that's where the similarity ended. Bill was convinced that freezing food would be the best way to preserve its nutrients. Paul felt that consumers would prefer a dry food. They argued the merits of each for hours on end.

Bill did not hesitate to share his knowledge of amino acids with his new friend. He discussed the difficulties involved in balancing the amino acids required by dogs and explained how he was using mink to obtain quick feedback. Paul was fascinated with this idea and seized on Bill's offer to visit Medina and tour the Bil-Jac operation.

When Paul returned to Dayton, he quietly bought three mink and put them in cages on the roof of his factory. But Paul had no experience handling mink and did not know thick gloves were needed to prevent them from chomping down on the hands that fed them. At the next dog show, Bill looked at Paul's fingers and recognized the bite marks. "I know what those are," he said to his friend. Thus began a healthy competition that led to a thirty-two-year partnership and a deep friendship that lasted until Paul's death in 2005.

Ch. Applewood Angus was an English Cocker Spaniel bred and owned by Mary M. Livezey and Jean S. LePoidevin. In the late 1970s, he was the top English Cocker Spaniel in the United States, winning eleven all-breed Best in Shows, fifty-one Sporting Group firsts, and Best of Breed in two national specialty shows (California and New York) while handled by Dick Becker. The dog was weaned on frozen Bil-Jac and later switched to dry Bil-Jac Select. He lived thirteen years and sired fifty champions. Ch. Applewood Angus is shown here in a 1979 painting by Prudence Walker.

A NO-LOSE SITUATION . . . .

In the mid-1960s, handler Dick Becker found himself in a lucky situation he could not explain. He had taken an English Cocker Spaniel, an English Setter, and a Pointer to a show in Harrisburg, Pennsylvania, and he just couldn't lose.

"We went before a judge from Australia and won with every dog we put in front of him," says Dick.

When the show was over, the judge came up to Dick and said, "I really like the condition of your dogs;

they have good muscle tone. So many American dogs are too soft and fluffy. I suspect it's because they are fed so much biscuit [gluten meal–based food]."

Dick told the judge he fed his dogs a frozen food made by a small company in Ohio. Unlike other dog foods, it contained fresh meat. "That's the key. It's high in digestible protein, and I can feel it in the muscle in your dogs," the judge said.

Bill and Paul decided to combine their interests in a partnership they called Kelly-Iams, which conducted research in amino acids to determine how the nutrition in animal foods altered with various ingredients. Their goal was to find ideal sources of quality protein and to identify which sources and combinations of sources best suited particular animals. They also evaluated how the proteins were affected by different processing techniques by examining and dissecting competitors' products.

At about the same time, Beatrice Foods purchased a company called Ross-Wells, which processed frozen chicken in their Berlin, Maryland, plant and shipped it to manufacturers of dog and mink food throughout the country. At this time, mink farmers traditionally fed their animals a wet food twice daily, which was both labor-intensive and messy. It was commonly believed that mink could not eat a dry food. Beatrice was hoping to prove them wrong.

Bill Ross and Loyal Wells knew and respected Bill Kelly as a result of a mink food supplement Bill had developed, and they hired Kelly-Iams to tackle the job. Bill and Paul put their heads together and came up with a drying process that produced a pellet-type food, which did not require refrigeration and was clean. This enabled a hopper to be filled with pellets that the mink could nibble as often as they wished. The mink loved its taste.

From left to right, Bob Kelly, Paul Iams, Ray Kelly, and Jim Kelly.

"A formula that is not fully digested results in a messy stool. A high-quality, nutritious food produces a small amount of dry stool and a luxurious, shiny coat," Bill explains.

"Although mink and dogs are both carnivores, their protein requirements are very different. You need 40 percent protein to put a proper coat on a mink. This is too much protein for a dog—it would destroy their kidneys. Dogs don't need as much protein, because their longer digestive tract allows them to assimilate less protein over a longer period of time. However, the protein they get still needs to be high quality. You could feed our 27-percent-protein dog food to a mink and get a good stool due to the quality of protein we use, but you would not get the ultimate coat. But if you take any other dog food that's made through the rendering process and feed it to a mink, the mink won't survive," he says.

In 1974, Bill and Paul decided to take their mink food to Norway, the world's largest mink producer. Because chicken was uncommon in the country and fish was abundant, the food had to be reformulated with fish proteins. Bill crossed the ocean with multiple formulas and visited 250 Norwegian mink ranchers, who agreed to test them on their animals. Over a period of about five years, they weeded out the formulas until they arrived at twenty strong candidates. The nutritional profiles of these formulas were analyzed to determine the most effective amino acid pattern. The key ingredient was herring.

Bill and Paul decided to build a plant in a small town in southern Norway to produce their herring-based mink food. The food was a big hit. However, Kelly-Iams ran into an unforeseen labor issue that nearly brought the project to a halt before the first batch was made.

"After the plant in Norway was partly built, we suddenly realized that the laws would only allow us to operate from 7:00 a.m. until 5:00 p.m.," says Bill. "There was no way we could run that plant only ten hours a day, because the fish we used for the mink food were only available for 120 days a year, so we had to produce a year's supply in four months."

Bill spent a great deal of time with Norwegian legislators, who were anxious to see the new venture succeed. Finally, logic prevailed. "It took almost a year, but we were the first company in that country ever to get two shifts," says Bill. The plant was a huge success and attracted attention to the owners' expertise in nutrition.

Some of the Norwegian mink farmers raised salmon on the side, utilizing the deep fjords that never froze to produce tons of tasty fish a year, primarily for salmon lovers in the United States. One day at lunch in Oslo, Bill learned that the salmon hatcheries were losing about 38 percent of their fingerlings. The farmers were in despair. Bill immediately suspected that poor nutrition was taking its toll on the young salmon. "You had better look at your formula," he advised the farmers.

Although Bill knew nothing about the nutritional needs of salmon, he was willing to help. He accompanied a group of farmers to a hatchery, where he analyzed the carcasses of several fish to determine their nutritional state. Bill had guessed correctly. "They just didn't have the right balance of food. The salmon were starving to death. Their systems were highly stressed," he says.

Bill set to work improving the fish food formula and in less than six months, fingerling loss had dropped from 38 percent to less than 7 percent.

For fourteen years, Bill and Paul went back and forth to Norway. They found the people to be kind and the work rewarding. However, the venture was tedious and had taken them off track. Through it all, neither man had lost his interest in making dog food. Finally, with their work in Norway complete, they decided to return to the United States and concentrate on feeding dogs.

Chapter 7 ....

REFINING PRODUCTION

By the late 1960s, the dry mink-food business was well underway in Maryland when Ross-Wells asked Bill and Paul to develop a formula for a dog food that would be made in the same plant. They called the dog food Eukanuba, an expression borrowed from jazz musicians meaning "the best." While the original Iams food was made in Dayton from rendered meal, Eukanuba contained fresh chicken meat and organs and was vacuum-dried. The process had been developed by Dr. Robert Bingham, a biochemist and food scientist that Beatrice Foods had hired as their head of agricultural products research. Bob Bingham hit it off with Bill and Paul right away.

"I was impressed with them as individuals and impressed with their philosophy of nutrition," Bingham says. "They understood how digestible an ingredient was and could predict what would happen when it was used."

Only two-and-a-half years after Bingham began working for Beatrice Foods, he was lured away by a competitor. Bill never forgot him, though, and in 1976 invited him to join Bil-Jac to work on developing a dry dog food.

"Our main challenge was to find a process that wouldn't damage protein. The only way was vacuum drying. It is more difficult to do, requires more equipment and effort, and is a more expensive process. That's why competitors take a cheaper route. They buy rendered meal that has the fat taken out, mix it with water or a minimal amount of fresh meat, and force it through equipment at high temperatures and pressures

Ch. Drycreek Chuggin Down the Line ("Spencer"), shown handled by Betty Jo Patterson, is the son of Ch. Whipperinn Virgil J. Shortly after birth, Spencer was kept alive by Bil-Jac mixed with milk after his mother contracted an infection and had to stop nursing her puppies. Photo by Kurtis Photography.

NOTHING SHORT OF A MIRACLE

Ch. Whipperinn Virgil J ("Virgil") is the winningest English Foxhound of all time, with fifty-five Best in Shows. Virgil's son Ch. Drycreek Chuggin Down the Line ("Spencer") has the same snappy looks and easygoing personality that made his father famous. By all accounts, Spencer is a miracle. Three days after he was born in May 2005, his mother developed an infection, which she transmitted to the puppies. The effect was immediate and devastating.

Jack and Betty Jo Patterson recall coming home from dinner that warm summer night and checking on the litter, which had appeared happy and healthy only a few hours earlier. "The mother was so sick she could not raise her head, and two of the six puppies had died," Jack recalls.

The shocked family was able to keep their wits about them and take lifesaving action. Jack called the vet while his wife began working on one of the tiny pups by rubbing it briskly and blowing in its nose. Within a few minutes, the vet arrived and gave each deathly ill dog a shot of antibiotics.

"He said we'd lose the whole litter," Betty Jo recalls.

The Pattersons had to be resourceful to save the remaining four puppies. Because their mother could no longer nurse them, they took Bil-Jac, put it in a blender with milk, and fed the puppies by hand. "They licked it off our fingers," says Betty Jo.

Amazingly, all four puppies and their mother survived, none the worse for their brush with death. One of the puppies was Spencer, who now carries the lineage of his champion father.

"We gave them other medicine, of course, but Bil-Jac was the main source of nutrition that kept them alive," says Betty Jo.

that take the molten mass and pop it. It is dried into a chunk and sprayed with rendered fat for flavor," Bingham explains. "We have natural fat distributed throughout our product. Ours is fresher, and the fresh fat and fresh protein are better for the dog."

As head of veterinary relations at Bil-Jac, Bingham taught third-year veterinary medicine students how Bil-Jac is made and why the process and ingredients are important. Today, his son Allen carries on this tradition. His other son, Lynn, is an equipment and process engineer at Bil-Jac.

Bingham also became involved in conducting research on Bil-Jac at Cornell's College of Veterinary Medicine. "We had several dogs with cancer that wouldn't eat. We tried Bil-Jac, and they ate it. It didn't cure the cancer, but it extended their life and quality of life," he remembers. "We also fed Bil-Jac to puppies with a predisposition for SIDS and pulled them through."

• •

Bil-Jac became the first distributor of Eukanuba outside the Dayton area in 1969 and retained the distributorship until the early 1990s. Meanwhile, frozen Bil-Jac continued to be made in Medina, Ohio. Bill was convinced his product offered superior nutrition to any other dog food and concentrated on marketing it directly to consumers to avoid the high cost of advertising. This meant Bill needed to put himself in front of as many potential customers as he could. Talks to area kennel clubs were valuable opportunities because club members were seriously interested in their dogs' health and were eager to hear Bill's views on nutrition.

Larry Taft and Bill Kelly

Larry Taft and his wife attended meetings of a local German Shepherd club. Typical of breed-specific clubs, their monthly meetings provided opportunities for social interaction as well as education. Taft volunteered to speak to his group about Bil-Jac, but the members weren't interested: They wanted Bill, and he was happy to oblige.

"I would have told them the same things Bill did, but it was very important to them to get information from someone high up in a company, not just a sales- man," says Taft.

Bill often took his sons to these meetings. Bill and Ruth had had three boys. Bob was born in 1946 and Ray in 1947, while the couple lived in an upstairs apartment in the Kelly family home- stead. A few years later, Bill and Ruth rented a single-family house in Grangerburg. In 1959 they built a ranch house on the lot next door to the homestead to accommodate their growing family, which by then included Jim.

Bob and Ray Kelly in front of the Bil-Jac delivery truck.

Bob remembers well accompanying his father to kennel club talks. "I was probably ten or twelve years old when Dad began taking one or two of us along," says Bob, now the president of Bil-Jac. "Almost every time he'd give a talk, he would say, 'You know, whenever I go see my doc- tor, I ask him why he doesn't ask me what I eat.'

He knew the way we eat has much to do with how healthy we are—and it's not just what we eat, it's how the food is prepared. He felt that if people understood this, they would understand there is a better way to make dog food."

There was no doubt Bil-Jac was different from anything that existed then or exists today. Over a period of more than sixty years the ingredi- ents have been continually refined to achieve the ideal combination and balance of amino acids. However, the basic philosophy has remained unchanged.

Bill visited local suppliers of beef and chicken, inspecting their plants and making arrangements to purchase select cuts and organs. He insisted the cuts be good enough to put on his own table.

Running Bil-Jac was time-consuming for both Bill and Ruth. Fortunately, both sets of grandparents lived in Medina and were able to help raise the children. For a while, Bill, Ruth, and the boys lived in an apartment above Bill's parents, Grace and Wil- liam (below), but Bob and Ray also saw their maternal grand- parents, Sarah and Clair Willey, several times a week (right).

"Meat deteriorates quickly, so it must be properly chilled and in the process of being turned into our product within a very few hours. We won't accept it if it's old or has been sitting around," he says.

Bill applied the same philosophy to the corn he used. Although meat is the primary source of protein in Bil-Jac, a small amount of carbohydrate is needed to provide energy. Bill chose freshly shelled corn from local farmers, which was ground to the proper texture and thoroughly cooked to convert the starch to a form of carbohydrate that dogs can utilize. Bill preferred corn over rice because it was much healthier for dogs.

Once the ground meat and cooked, ground corn were mixed, Bill's carefully researched formula of vitamins and minerals was added. These were balanced to the proper value of digestible nutrients.

While chunky dry dog foods made from tasteless rendered meal are sprayed with fat to make

them edible, it was never necessary to add fat to Bil-Jac. The freshly ground meat is naturally juicy, and freezing the food preserves this juiciness.

Turning out a dog food with unconventional production requirements was not easy. In 1958, Bill hired Wally Lamphear to manage the plant. It was a smart move; Wally proved to be an excellent manager and trained his capable brother-in-law, Walt Caskey; his son, Chuck; and his grandson,

Bob and Ray with their baby brother, Jim.

Bobby, in the Bil-Jac way of doing things. Bobby Lamphear has served as plant manager since 1976.

In the early days, producing Bil-Jac was hard work. All ingredients arrived by truck and were stacked on pallets and carted into a freezer. Bill visited the plant daily to make sure everything was working right and to lend a hand, if needed.

The employees loved and respected Bill, and the feeling was mutual. Bill showed tremendous respect for the people who shared his vision.

He considered them family and treated them accordingly.

"When you're the boss, you usually don't socialize with anybody you work with, but Bill had actual neighbors working in his company. They went bowling together. Ruth was friendly

Original Bil-Jac plant manager Wally Lamphear (third from left) with plant employees Harry Streck, Walter Khoenle, and Andy Haight in 1982.

with their wives. That usually doesn't happen," says Bobby Lamphear.

To this day, Bill knows everyone's name and never fails to inquire about how their families are doing. "In most companies nowadays, you're

a number. Bill makes you feel important," says Lamphear.

Bill's respectful attitude created a culture at Bil-Jac that made working there a joy. Everyone pulled together to make the best product possible. This meant concentrating on quality and never taking chances.

"It's an endless job to make sure everything is perfect. We don't skimp, we don't cut corners, and we don't take chances. We physically check every-thing—and I mean everything," says Lamphear.

Bill went directly to suppliers to explain how he expected the ingredients to be handled and to let them know what standards had to be met in order to sell ingredients to Bil-Jac. Suppliers that did not conform were crossed off the list and forced to sell their ingredients to pet food compa-nies with lower standards.

"The meat that goes into Bil-Jac is inspected by the USDA. That's unusual for dog food," Lamp-hear says.

Quality is further ensured by producing the food in batches, rather than on a continuous pro-duction line. This enables every product going into the food to be tested before production begins. The mixture is also tested periodically throughout production. Bill personally reviews the results of every batch produced to ensure it meets his strict standards.

The uniqueness of Bil-Jac processes has always posed a production problem. Because no other food was or is produced in this same manner, the machinery required to make Bil-Jac has never been available. Bil-Jac plant managers have had to tap their engineering skills to design and manufacture their own equipment. Over the years, the designs have been altered to arrive at machinery that meets the company's needs perfectly.

Preventive maintenance is done on an ongoing basis. "Believe it or not, we don't have breakdowns that stop production, and never have," says Lamphear.

Every night after the final batch has been bagged, the machinery, walls, and ceiling are thoroughly cleaned with 180-degree water and a foaming cleanser, which sits for ten minutes before being rinsed off. This is followed by sanitizer. Then the entire plant is hosed off with hot water before production begins again.

"Inspectors tell us our place is cleaner than human food factories. They say it's unreal what we do for dog food," says Lamphear with obvious pride.

Over the years, no real changes have been made in the way Bil-Jac frozen dog food is produced. The only significant development has been the addition of new dry food formulations for dogs of different ages and weights. The original frozen formula for Bil-Jac is an ideal food and appropri-

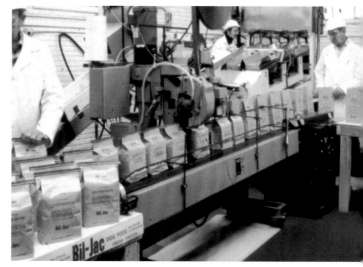

The Bil-Jac frozen food production line in 1980.

ate for dogs of all ages, weights, and breeds.

The development of specialty lines of Bil-Jac dry dog food has provided a source of constant amusement for Lamphear, who enjoys his reputation as a jokester.

"When people ask me what I do at Bil-Jac, I tell them, 'I'm the taste tester. When I was young, they put me on the Puppy line. As I got older, I started on the Select. Then I got overweight, so they put me on Reduced Fat. But now that I'm old, I'm on the Senior food,'" he says with characteristic good humor, adding that some people ask him if he's serious.

A job working with people you like, producing a product you respect, is a rare combination. It accounts for why Bil-Jac retains so many employees for decades, and why Bobby Lamphear hasn't missed a day's work in twenty-seven years. "You can't ask for nicer and more dedicated people, and that's worth a lot to me," he says.

Chapter 8

GROWING UP IN THE BUSINESS

Taking his boys to dog club talks to hear what was on the owners' minds was part of Bill's plan to ensure that his sons understood all aspects of the dog food business. His plan also included lessons in manufacturing and distribution.

"I can remember riding on the truck with Dad and Uncle Jack, too, in terrible weather and in great weather. We used to help them unload the food," says Bob, referring to himself and his younger brother Ray.

Growing up, the boys worked in the plant before school, on weekends, and during the summer. This instilled a work ethic and helped the boys learn how to make intelligent, independent decisions.

"Dad always said, 'Just ask yourself if it's the right thing to do,'" says Ray, now the vice president of Bil-Jac.

"I can remember getting up at 3:30 in the morning and going to work. We did the tough stuff, but a lot of what we did helped us understand what was right and what was wrong to do," says Bob.

Manufacturing started at 4:00 a.m. When they couldn't keep up with demand, the boys would return to the plant after making deliveries and run a couple more batches before filling the five- and two-pound bags by hand.

Summers were dedicated to working in the plant. Because they had limited space to store raw ingredients, manufacturing was done Monday through Thursday. On Friday, tractor trailers full of supplies for the following week would

FEEDING ATHLETES . . . .

Tulsa veterinarian Robert Green has been a passionate bird hunter his entire life. After he graduated from vet school and entered a practice, he scheduled his free time around hunting season.

In those days, Dr. Green owned three Pointers, a breed known to forget to eat in the excitement of doing the job they were bred to do. In fact, at the end of a season, many Pointers are skin and bones. But at the end of one particularly stressful two-month quail-hunting season in the mid-1970s, Dr. Green's dogs still looked robust. That's because he fortified them with Bil-Jac.

"We hunted twenty-four days that season. Sometimes we would go out three or four days in a row. It was very hard on the dogs," he says.

In an effort to ensure his dogs consumed enough calories to maintain their weight, Dr. Green initially tried feeding them a prescription diet created for guard dogs in Vietnam. It contained 50 percent fat—an enormous source of calories—but was nutritionally poor. His dogs failed to gain weight, and their stools were runny and smelly.

Then someone recommended he try Bil-Jac. It produced the results he wanted.

"My dogs performed well, and at the end of the season, they actually weighed more than when they started and were solid muscle," says Dr. Green. "Other foods pale in comparison."

Kissamee Blackthor Jax, owned by Debra Freidus, DVM, and Daniel Grabowski, was the American Pointer Club's Top Field Dog in 1999 and 2000.

arrive, and the boys would unload the rigs from 6:00 a.m. to 5:00 p.m. "It was hard work, but we always had fun doing it," Ray remembers. "Bobby Lamphear's grandfather was the manager, and he was a tremendous guy. He could get us to work, but we had fun with him. I know he meant the world to Dad, because he put up with an awful lot from us kids."

Although Bill's dedication to building his business was a full-time effort, every year the Kellys took a summer vacation. One year, they took the train from Cleveland to Detroit to go to the zoo. Other years they visited Niagara Falls or Pymatuning Lake.

One year, their aunt Mil and uncle Lloyd Simon and aunt Mary and uncle Tony Kasza invited the whole family to accompany them on a fishing trip to Canada. "It was the greatest vacation we ever had. We just loved it up there," says Ray.

A vacation meant that production had to be accelerated, or there would not be enough Bil-Jac to fill orders. The night before the Kellys left for vacation, Bill would work until dawn. His sacrifice was not lost on his boys.

"As a kid I thought, gosh, he's doing an awful lot just so we can go and take a vacation," says Ray.

The boys respected their father and didn't mind working for the family business. However, they naturally had mixed feelings about Bill's lack of materialism, particularly when faced with something as appealing as a new bicycle.

"I vividly remember growing up in a frame house in Grangerburg. A lot of our friends' parents had come through the War years and the Depression without a lot of stuff, so they gave their kids things they had never had when they were young," says Ray. "I remember a couple kids who had big picnics at Euclid Park. They got a lot of presents, new bikes and this and that. It's not like we didn't have bikes, but they weren't English racers. I thought those kids were so lucky. But you know, what Dad gave us in opportunities was priceless. Back then, we didn't look at it that way, but in hindsight, I'd much rather have the opportunities than a brand-new bicycle."

Bob Kelly building a soap box racer, which became the first advertisement for Bil-Jac.

Chapter 9 ....

THE KELLY BOYS BRANCH OUT

Although working at Bil-Jac became second nature to the Kelly boys, Bill did not press them to join the family business. Instead, he encouraged them to venture out and try their hand at different careers.

After high school, Bob attended Ohio University. Although he graduated with a business degree, he was unsure what direction he wanted to take. There was a tremendous shortage of teachers at that time, and the county superintendent talked him into going into education. It turned out to be a very good decision.

"I taught slow learners, and I absolutely loved it. It was so rewarding," Bob says with a smile. He also coached basketball and became the varsity basketball coach at Black River High School in Sullivan, Ohio, not far from Medina.

But in the spring of 1974, Bill asked Bob if he would consider coming to work for the family company. Beatrice Foods, which had bought out Ross-Wells, was interested in creating a vacuum-drying process. Bill hoped this new process would enable him to make a dry dog food as nutritious and tasty as frozen Bil-Jac. However, Bill was spread thin and could not devote enough time to making it happen. He was also having quality-control problems with mink food production at the plant and needed a reliable manager who understood the Bil-Jac philosophy.

"If there's any way I could talk you into going down there to work, I need somebody there every day to make sure that things are being done right," he told Bob.

Ch. Adesa I'm Stepping Out, shown winning Best of Breed in the Bernese Mountain Dog class at Westminster Kennel Club Show in 2007. Breeder and handler Bobbi Kinley-Blewett feeds all her dogs Bil-Jac, regardless of their breed. Bobbi learned about Bil-Jac from her parents, breeders of Afghan Hounds, German Shepherds, and Bernese Mountain Dogs. They feed it to their own dogs as well as to their clients' dogs, as does Bobbi's sister, who runs a boarding kennel.

NATURALLY GOOD

Bobbi Kinley-Blewett was born into the dog show world. Her parents, Carolyn and Bob Kinley, bred and showed Afghan Hounds, German Shepherds, and Bernese Mountain Dogs. Bobbi inherited their love of dogs and has bred and shown Bernese for many years.

Over the past three decades, the Kinleys have had many winners. One of Carolyn's dogs was the first Bernese to win the working group at Westminster and went on to be the top-winning Bernese in history. Bobbi has had the number one Bernese in the country since 1999 with several different dogs.

All Kinley-bred dogs have been raised on Bil-Jac.

"I like it because it's a natural food. Because Bernese Mountain Dogs have a high rate of cancer, I think it's important not to take unnecessary risks with their diet," says Bobbi. Fortunately, the dogs love the food that's good for them.

"The problem I run into is that Bernese Mountain Dogs dive into the Bil-Jac and eat it so fast that it gets stuck in the corners of the bowl. Then they pick up the bowl, carry it all over the place, and end up throwing it around trying to get that last little bit of Bil-Jac. It's hilarious and very noisy," Bobbi says with a laugh.

Despite his love for teaching and coaching, Bob heeded his father's call and moved to Maryland. It was a difficult decision that he made reluctantly. On the positive side, the timing was right: Bob had gotten married a couple of years earlier and was living on a shoestring. By moving to Maryland, he tripled his salary, which made the career change much easier.

It did not take long for Bob to prove his worth, and after about one year on the job, he was named manager of the entire complex. Under Bob's leadership, the Maryland operation thrived, producing dry dog foods under the Eukanuba label.

"The first few years Iams's Eukanuba was manufactured, we made every pound of it in that plant. We put Eukanuba on the map, because it was the first dog food made this way," he says, referring to the vacuum-drying process.

In 1979, Bill asked Bob to return to their Ohio headquarters. After Bob left Maryland, Beatrice Foods continued to operate the plant. However, new management began cutting corners. As a result, the quality of their products suffered dramatically, and the plant began losing money. When the Kellys heard the plant was about to shut down, they bought it.

"It took us a year and a half to get it back to the way we wanted it, but it was the best thing we ever did. It enabled us to make a dry dog food that is so close to our frozen product that we can ship it internationally. Because it is shelf-stable, it is a lot easier to manage and sell than a frozen product," Bob says.

Today, Bob Kelly is president of Bil-Jac and Kelly Foods, the dry dog food and treats subsidiary. For the most part, he concentrates on manufacturing, although the three Kelly boys share all responsibilities involved in the manufacturing, distribution, and sales of all their products. "We probably spend more time on manufacturing and ingredients than we do on selling, because we can't spend millions of dollars in advertising. All our major competitors are owned by big conglomerates with deep pockets. We have to concentrate on making a better product, and that's done by making sure our ingredients are procured the right way and that we are manufacturing right," Bob explains.

The secret to creating a dry dog food that preserves the nutrients was the answer to a long-held dream.

"People always used to ask Dad why he didn't sell a dry dog food, and his answer was, 'I'm not going to sell a dry dog food unless I can be sure that I can present the nutrients to the animal in the same way that I can with my frozen food,'" says Bob.

Bill struggled for more than thirty years to accomplish this goal, finally settling on a method of dehydrating fresh meat in a way that does not damage the heat-sensitive amino acids of a protein. The typical way meat protein is dehydrated in the pet food industry is through rendering. Leftover meat products not suitable for human consumption are picked up by truck. The meat is not chilled, so it does not stay fresh. At the rendering plant, it is cooked at a high temperature to destroy bacteria. The fat is melted off, and the meal is dehydrated at temperatures of 280 to 300 degrees. The result is a relatively tasteless powder that is reconstituted with water and sprayed with fat to give it some taste.

In contrast, dry Bil-Jac is made from fresh chicken. And to the Kellys, fresh means fresh.

"Because we've been making a frozen food for years, we know what fresh means. It can't be a little bit fresh—it's fresh, or we don't use it," says Bob.

A 6,000-pound batch of dry Bil-Jac begins with 8,400 pounds of fresh chicken and organ meat. Because the meat is 75 to 80 percent moisture, it is dehydrated before being mixed with carbohydrates, fiber, and vitamins. Bil-Jac's unique vacuum process enables the food to be dehydrated at only 165 degrees, which does not damage the heat-sensitive proteins.

"It has been revolutionary for us. Our food is so much healthier and more palatable than everybody else's. And because dogs' senses are so much keener than ours, they can tell when something is fresh and processed right. That's why dogs love to eat Bil-Jac," says Bob.

Thanks to Bil-Jac's unique production methods, all forms of dry Bil-Jac are as tasty and nutritious as the frozen formulation.

Chapter 10 ....

GROWING PAINS

Although Ray Kelly was initiated into the Bil-Jac culture by working weekends and summers in the plant, he was not initially interested in joining the family business. Instead, his goal was to become a teacher. He spent two years at Rio Grande College (now called the University of Rio Grande) in southern Ohio before transferring to the University of Akron. Like his brother Bob, he ended up teaching special education students.

"You knew you could make a difference," Ray says.

In the summer of 1972, Bill asked Ray if he would consider joining the family business. Ray thought long and hard before saying yes. "I loved teaching. It was a hard decision to leave, but it was the right decision," he says.

In his new position at Bil-Jac, Ray was responsible for increasing sales. He found it a pleasure, because he was so proud of the product. "We know we can feed a dog better than anyone else can. We have a great message, but marketing and advertising are so expensive today that we can't get caught up in that game. We have to figure out other ways to reach customers. It's an everyday challenge, but I like doing what we're doing, and we're successful," Ray says. "I have a lot of friends who hate getting up and going to work on Mondays, but I get antsy on Sunday night just wanting to get in here."

The key to new as well as repeat sales of Bil-Jac lies in the quality of the product. No other dog food can assure customers of quality like Bil-Jac can. "It probably sounds a little bit hokey, but

Ch. Whipperinn Virgil J ("Virgil") is the top-winning English Foxhound of all time. His owners attributed his legendary coat to a Bil-Jac diet. Photo by Kurtis Photography.

NOTHING TO HIDE ....

A Valentino among dogs, Jack and Betty Jo Patterson's English Foxhound, Ch. Whipperinn Virgil J ("Virgil"), was so handsome that he turned heads wherever he went. A good-looking man can engender jealousy among competitors, and it's no different in the dog world. It wasn't long before people began to suggest that Virgil's spectacular coat had perhaps been "enhanced."

About one year after Virgil began his career, the Pattersons were preparing him to enter a class at a show in Buffalo when a handler named Andrew Green approached Patterson. Andrew's father, Peter Green, is one of the world's most respected dog show handlers and judges.

"Did you know there's a big debate going on about the Virgil dog? Everybody says you dye him. That's why his black saddle is so black and so bright," Green said to Patterson.

As Virgil's hairdresser, Patterson knew for sure he had nothing to hide.

"Let's end that debate," he responded without hesitation. "Take this dog to your dad and put him on your table. Get down to the base of the hair, then come back and tell me if he's dyed."

A short time later, Green returned with the dog, admitting the naysayers were wrong.

"Look, Andrew, if I could dye dogs to look like this, I'd be doing it for a living," Patterson joked. "Virgil's coat is lustrous and rich because he was raised on Bil-Jac. It gives the color life."

Photo by Kurtis Photography

we're not driven by the dollar as much as we are by doing things the right way. We spend more time making sure our raw ingredients are purchased and handled right than we do selling the product, because that's where quality starts and stops," Ray explains.

Although Bil-Jac is not immune to tough economic times, the Kellys refuse to take shortcuts that could compromise the quality of their products. "Like other companies, we tighten our belt, look over our shoulder, and make sure we're as efficient as we possibly can be. But the breeding community, which has been the backbone of our business for years, would know immediately if we started cheapening things. We have very loyal customers, the type who will give up their simple luxuries to keep feeding the family dog, and we don't want to do anything to disappoint them," Ray says.

Initially, Bil-Jac was sold through independent pet food supply stores. The Kellys provided small freezer cases similar to those used for ice cream bars and delivered directly to the stores. Then about twenty years ago, pet superstores appeared across the country. Without a national distribution system, Bil-Jac had no cost-effective or practical method of distributing their frozen dog food to pet stores outside a reasonable driving distance from the plant in which it was made. Grocery stores were the answer. In some markets, the Kellys were able to arrange for distributors of frozen foods to deliver Bil-Jac to grocery stores. It's an ideal situation, but one that almost never happened, because Bill originally was not interested in having grocery stores carry his product. He was very pleased serving the specialty niche of pet food stores. But a serendipitous event changed his mind.

In 1967, a temporary Bil-Jac driver substituting for a vacationing employee attempted to make a Friday delivery to Sam Rego, a Cleveland-area grocer who owned German Shepherds. When he arrived at the Rego home, he found it buzzing with party preparations. Because the freezers and refrigerators were chock-full of food for guests, Mrs. Rego told the driver to take the frozen food to their grocery store, where she would pick it up on Monday.

The driver did as he was instructed and delivered the dog food to Rego's. However, no one alerted the store that the delivery was coming. A stock clerk priced the Bil-Jac and put it out for sale. When Mrs. Rego went to pick up her dog food a few days later, every bag had been sold.

Naturally, Rego's wanted to carry Bil-Jac. Soon, Pick 'n Pay wanted it, too. Heinen's and Buehler's followed. The Kellys struggled to keep up with the demand, and it took a while to gear up production and delivery to meet the needs of so many stores. But this wasn't fast enough for some grocers, who had witnessed the product flying off their competitors' shelves.

One night Ray was cleaning up the warehouse when there was a knock on the door. He opened it to find a man in a suit, who introduced himself as a buyer from Heinen's. He said he had tried unsuccessfully to reach someone by phone, so he had driven out in person to tell them he was interested in carrying Bil-Jac. Ray assured him that he would give his business card to the right person.

Many years later when Ray was calling on Heinen's, the same man related the story of how he drove out to Bil-Jac and had to talk to the janitor. Ray explained that he was that janitor, and the two men had a good laugh.

Today, many grocery stores outside Northern Ohio also carry frozen Bil-Jac, and negotiations with multistate grocery chains are underway. In every grocery store where Bil-Jac is sold, it is a top seller among frozen foods, often coming in second only to the most popular brand of orange juice.

"With these numbers, it's easy to go into a new grocery chain and make the first sale. But to get the second sale, we have to have sold people on our product. If we don't do due diligence, our product would just sit there, since Bil-Jac is not sold in the pet food section. Once people try Bil-Jac, however, they always come back for more," Ray explains.

• •

Although it was problematic for pet specialty stores to sell frozen Bil-Jac, the dry dog food was an option for them. The Kellys hired two experts who shared their philosophies and values to expand this area of the market. Brit Hyde and Tim Viancourt had worked at Smucker's, another family business with a stellar reputation. Both men were only interested in selling a product that was different and better than anything in the industry. Bil-Jac fit the bill.

Today, Bil-Jac dry dog food and treats are only sold through the pet specialty channel, which consists of retailers such as PetSmart, Petco, Pet Supplies Plus, regional chains, and thousands of independent pet specialty retailers across the country.

"The pet specialty segment of our business, while extremely competitive, has been a major growth area for Bil-Jac over the past twenty years," says Viancourt.

• •

For a family-owned business competing against conglomerates, continued growth requires innovative marketing techniques. The dog foods that compete with Bil-Jac are owned by multinational corporations with seemingly bottomless advertising budgets. These brands include Purina, owned by Nestlé; Hill's, which was purchased by Colgate-Palmolive; and Iams and Eukanuba, which were acquired by Proctor & Gamble in 1999. Del Monte owns many of the well-known grocery store brands, including Kibbles 'n Bits, Nature's Recipe, and Gravy Train. M&M/Mars is now a pet food conglomerate in its own right, owning Pedigree, Nutro, and Royal Canin. These multi-billion-dollar corporations market to dog owners primarily through television commercials and coupons.

Bil-Jac attracts customers primarily through in-store demonstrations, which provide opportunities to tell the Bil-Jac story directly to consumers. "We can prove that dogs prefer our product, and the results speak for themselves," says Viancourt. Bil-Jac knows its consumers will listen because Bil-Jac cares about customers' pets. "We target the type of people who are really concerned about their animals and consider themselves their dog's companion, not necessarily the other way around. PetSmart calls them *pet parents*. Their attitude is, 'These are my kids, and there's nothing I won't do for them,'" says Viancourt.

Bil-Jac makes customers an introductory offer that eliminates the risk of trying out the food: Buy any size bag and get a free challenge pack. This enables the owner to conduct a two-bowl challenge without opening the bag. The results are 100 percent guaranteed. Since dogs always prefer the fresh taste of Bil-Jac, unopened bags rarely get returned. Customers also get a coupon toward their next purchase.

"We tell people we put our money into the food and the introductory offer instead of into advertising, and that they will see how much their dog

loves eating this product," says Viancourt. "We want them to go home and have that 'Voila!' moment when they do the two-bowl challenge and realize we were telling the truth and there really is something different about Bil-Jac."

That's how Bil-Jac continues to grow, customer by satisfied customer. "I'll tell you that it's our commitment to the heritage of the product and the quality of the product that enables us not only to grow and survive, but also to thrive in a very challenging, very competitive business. We might never get to be the biggest, but we continue to grow. We are a very healthy company and have a product that nobody else knows how to make," says Viancourt.

Lacking the deep advertising pockets of competitors' multinational corporate owners, Bil-Jac continues to be marketed through breeders, trainers, and in-store demonstrations, rather than through conventional ads and commercials. In the 1980s, however, the Kellys did run television commercials in Northern Ohio for a short time. The commercials featured popular local television personality Jan Jones, shown in this 1982 photo with Bill, Ray, Jim, and Bob Kelly at Bil-Jac's thirty-fifth anniversary celebration at the Western Reserve Kennel Club Show.

BUILDING NEW MARKETS

By the time Jim Kelly graduated from Wittenberg University in 1980, Bob and Ray had laid the groundwork for Bil-Jac sales outside Northern Ohio. Like his older brothers, Jim had been initiated into the inner workings of his family's business at an early age. But rather than pursuing a different career first, Jim always wanted to work at Bil-Jac. He graduated on a Saturday and started as a Bil-Jac driver/salesman the following Monday.

"I never felt pressured to join the business, but I had learned enough to know that other opportunities were not as good. I was familiar with the product, knew how good it was, and knew it was easy to get people to try it," Jim says.

At first, he accompanied Larry Taft on sales calls. It was an important lesson on the value of human connections. "Larry had phenomenal relationships with all kinds of customers—store owners, breeders, kennels, and vets. You can try and sell all you want, but relationships make it so much easier," says Jim.

Taft was a good talker, but he also knew when to keep his ears open and his mouth shut. "He told me to listen to what the customer was saying

Larry Taft with Bil-Jac's new sales van, purchased in 1973.

WAXED PAPER BAG ....

Ever since the first batch of frozen Bil-Jac was made for sale, it has been packaged in brown waxed paper bags with red lettering. The wax coating helps preserve Bil-Jac's freshness, and the simple bag distinguishes it from competitors' more colorful packaging.

A couple of years ago, Ray Kelly was looking through a pile of packaging trade magazines when he spotted one with a photo of a plain brown bag on the cover. The copy read, "Do you think you can sell a product in this?"

Ray put the magazine on his father's desk with a note saying, "What do you think?"

It gave them both a big chuckle.

"We are identified with that waxed paper bag," says Ray. "Over the years, we have asked numerous market research companies whether we should update the package look or not. They always say, 'You have an icon here. Don't change anything.'"

Bil-Jac packages its frozen dog food in a bag resembling the one it used in 1947. No other dog food has similar packaging.

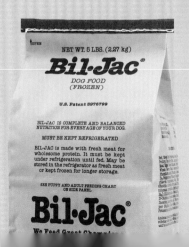

and to learn their language and questions. This was an eye-opener for me," says Jim. "I learned that stores wanted to know how we could help them move the product. Breeders, kennel owners, and vets wanted to know the nutritional difference between Bil-Jac and other products," he explains.

Jim worked in Northern Ohio for a couple of years, gradually introducing Bil-Jac to the Youngstown market. By 1983 he was ready to strike out on his own. He loaded a van with Bil-Jac and clothes and set out for southern Ohio, where he made cold calls to build accounts and handled sales and delivery. In one year, his route grew large enough to import a driver from Medina.

The first employees Jim hired in the southern Ohio market were close friends who, like Jim, had grown up working at Bil-Jac during their summer vacations. One was Dave Pelot, who still works for Bil-Jac in Florida.

Jim gradually moved on to Columbus, then to Dayton, the home of Iams. In a short time, he enlarged the Dayton staff to six.

It was an exciting time to be in Dayton. Paul Iams had sold the company to a former employee named Clay Mathile. Mathile was a marketing genius who turned the Iams brand into a common household name. Bil-Jac was still distributing Iams products through the arrangement Bill and Paul had made at Kelly-Iams. This enabled Jim to attend Iams sales meetings, where he learned how the competition marketed its product.

"I saw how big money-spenders worked. Iams was very big on merchandising and had their own displays and color-coded bags. I learned how they billboarded their products," Jim remembers.

The opportunity enabled him to capitalize on Iams's weaknesses and his own product's strengths. As a result, some of his most memorable career achievements occurred in Dayton, including the day he convinced the premier kennel in Dayton, which was founded in 1947, to switch to Bil-Jac.

"You could eat off the floors, it was so clean," Jim says about the kennel. The owners had been very loyal to one brand of dog food, but Jim kept stopping in to talk with them. After about a year, they understood the merits of Bil-Jac and made the switch. Now they are loyal to Bil-Jac. "They have fed nothing else since the mid-1980s," Jim says.

One major advantage Bil-Jac had over larger companies was the ability to provide personal service: They delivered to homes. "Dave Pelot knew where the keys were hidden, and he would let himself in and put the food in the freezer," says Jim, who was even known to deliver food on Thanksgiving Day. "We took care of customers. When they needed food, we got it to them."

During the time Jim was in Dayton, Bil-Jac introduced its dry dog food to the market. For the first time, Iams felt threatened. Bil-Jac's frozen formulation had been a differentiating factor, but Clay Mathile felt the dry formula put Bil-Jac in direct competition with both Iams and Eukanuba. As a result, the association between Iams and Bil-Jac was no longer to his company's advantage, and he ended the relationship.

"The divorce wasn't nasty. It was just time for us to part company," says Jim.

• •

In addition to calling on pet food stores, Jim and his staff introduced Bil-Jac to pet owners at town festivals and home and garden shows. "We worked every weekend and ran ourselves ragged, but we got our samples out there," he says.

Gradually, the dry food caught on, and Jim's hardworking crew was able to back off as con-sumers began pouring into pet food superstores to buy it.

After eight years in southern Ohio, Jim moved back to Medina to help develop a national distribution system for the dry food. Although it sounds like a relatively straightforward project, the competitors had the large distributors locked up. Bil-Jac was beginning to make a serious dent in their business, and the competitors did not hesitate to throw around their muscle. When rebel distributors in the Carolinas decided to supply Bil-Jac, Iams pulled its products.

Big-box stores put additional pressure on distributors. One way they are able to keep prices low is to cut out the middleman. Jim had to find a way to distribute Bil-Jac to PetSmart stores nationwide without using a warehouse as a hub. The transition took several years. Today, Bil-Jac has its own distribution in New England, the Carolinas, Georgia, Texas, and Oklahoma.

With the logistics worked out, Jim returned to marketing, his primary interest and college major. He continues to look for innovative ways to reach customers. To date, in-store demonstrations have proven to be the most efficient, effective, and cost-effective way of getting the word out. "It's easy to get a conversation going.

Customers will pull out their wallets and show me photos of their dog," he says. "People love their animals, and we love the fact we can make them better. We are definitely as passionate about making them better as they are passionate about their animals."

Jim's only regret is that the business is evolving so fast he is no longer able to cultivate the friendships he found so valuable.

"I miss the days of calling on mom-and-pop shops. I miss the relationships. Those are going away," he says sadly.

Chapter 12

ALL IN THE FAMILY

It is unusual today to find a family business run by family members who are content to focus their individual strengths and diverse personalities on a common goal, but that's how Bil-Jac works. Bob attributes this collective ability to his father's wisdom and guidance. "If we heard it once, we heard it a number of times; many family businesses don't work when they get into the second generation. Dad wanted to make sure that wasn't going to happen. He told us if we worked hard, people would trust us," Bob says, adding they had to prove themselves trustworthy and hardworking to each other, as well.

Fortunately, the Kelly boys are versatile, flexible, and familiar with all aspects of the business. Therefore, they do not experience the jealousy or territorialism that can tear a family business apart.

"There is so much to do that we have no problem dividing the responsibilities. We have individual projects, but there's nothing we don't talk to each other about. We realize communication is extremely important," says Bob.

As Bil-Jac has grown, the family of employees has grown with it. It is clear the Kellys know how to identify the right employees and retain them. From the very start, Bill never called those who worked alongside him "employees;" they were "associates" whom he considered part of the Bil-Jac family. This attitude of respect has lasted for more than sixty years and is responsible for the longevity of most employees.

Ch. Brunswig's Cryptonite, pictured here with handler George Murray, winning Best of Breed at the Doberman Pinscher Club of America Show. When Cryptonite arrived in Murray's care, the experienced handler felt the dog's coat was not show quality. The nutrition in Bil-Jac brought out the coat's color and richness. In the following three-and-a-half years, Cryptonite won 393 Best of Breeds and 124 Best in Shows.

IMPROVING ON PERFECTION ....

As a professional dog handler, George Murray did not think it was necessary to see a client's dog before it arrived on his doorstep, since most dogs arrived ready to compete. That's why he was surprised when Ch. Brunswig's Cryptonite stepped out of his cage. The red Doberman had won two Best in Shows by the age of fourteen months, but at twenty-three months, his coat needed a lot of work.

"The color needed to be darker and richer," Murray says.

As the owner of a fifty-run boarding kennel in Brooklyn, Michigan, Murray had long used Bil-Jac for his boarders as well as for his show dogs. He knew dogs loved the taste and thrived on the nutrition. "My boarders always wondered why their dogs seemed happier at my place than at other kennels. It's because they ate so well," he says.

Murray started feeding Cryptonite Bil-Jac, and in no time at all, the dog's coat was a shiny dark color. Cryptonite was shown 428 times during the next three-and-a-half years and won Best of Breed in 92 percent of the shows. He had 350 group placements (89 percent), of which 258 were group firsts (74 percent). He also won 124 Best in Shows, which means nearly half the time he won the Working Group, he was also named Best in Show.

"Shoulder placement was his forte. He had a magnificent chest," says Murray. "But of course, a dog's condition is very important, too, so we toned him and improved his coat with Bil-Jac."

"People make you. If you treat them right, they will usually do right by you," says Bill.

Working for Bil-Jac has another advantage over working for other companies—it's fun. "We grew up knowing every employee. Many of them were truly like aunts and uncles. They would sled with us after work or go bowling with my parents. We always said, if it's not fun, it's work," says Jim with a chuckle. "I think it really pleases Dad that people like to work for him. I don't think he thinks of it as working for him. He is a real people guy."

"We have many valuable people who work for us," adds Bob. "They put their hearts into their work, just like we do. When you have that kind of people, you need to take care of them."

In a way, Bil-Jac is a throwback to more compassionate days. "We are part of a company that is unique and different. Companies that are committed to their employees don't exist anymore," says Tim Viancourt. "It's not that we're the highest paid. It's the intangibles, the concern for each other. The Kellys are very, very committed, and it permeates throughout the organization."

The result is a sense of dynamism and flexibility that flies in the face of that all-too-common saying, "It's not in my job description." All Bil-Jac employees do far more than their titles suggest.

"You pick up whatever hat you have to wear and you do the job, because you're passionately committed to the company," says Bob.

Take Chief Financial Officer Jo Anne Duncan, for example, who is involved in some aspect or another of just about everything happening at Bil-Jac. In addition to her financial duties, she managed all aspects of the design and construction of Bil-Jac's new Medina headquarters, which opened in 2006. The unconventional office building has the warmth and appearance of a traditional home, which appropriately reflects the noncorporate attitude of the Bil-Jac family. In 2007, Jo Anne spent many months at the Maryland plant working with processes and production flow. She also serves as Bil-Jac's de facto

In 2006 Bil-Jac Foods opened its new corporate headquarters in Medina, Ohio, only a few miles from the home where Bill Kelly had developed and sold the first bags of Bil-Jac in 1947.

information technology person, simply because she understands computers.

"She is a doer. She is organized and can keep a lot of balls in the air," says Bob about Jo Anne. "I'd put her up against any CFO in any company in this country. She's that valuable," he says, adding that "she's way more than a CFO to us."

"We don't have a lot of management layers, but the Kellys are willing to give you projects and show their confidence that you can handle challenges," says Jo Anne. "Bill really feels it's his job to nurture the people who work for him and let them make mistakes, because that's how they're going to learn," she says. "When you

Over the years, Bil-Jac has been widely admired but never imitated.

put in the hours, it's not taken for granted that it's something you have to do. They sincerely appreciate it."

Although Jo Anne has little direct contact with the product on a daily basis, she shows the same respect for it that she would if she were in production or sales. She admires the fact that Bill still comes to the office every day to conduct quality control.

"He monitors the quality of every single batch produced at every plant. He is always wondering if there is a better way to do something—not a more profitable way, but a better way to enhance the food by tweaking the formula. The Kellys truly want the best product for pets," she says.

But in a company where "better" can mean "more expensive," she struggles with their ongoing quest for quality.

"From a finance person's point of view, it can sometimes be frustrating when they say, 'We're going to spend a little bit more money to make this ingredient even better.' I'll think, *Why do we have to get the very best? We already make the best food. Isn't that good enough?*"

But it never is. And one fact is indisputable: Sales of Bil-Jac continue to climb every year. The Kellys' gamble that dog owners would prefer quality if they had a choice has paid off. "We can't compete with the big guys in media, so we compete on results," Jo Anne explains.

Despite running a solid, profitable company, none of the Kellys live a lavish lifestyle. Instead, they refocus their profits into building the business. "They truly want the best environment possible for their employees and want to make sure the company continues to make money and is solid for the employees and for them. It's very nice to see," says Jo Anne.

Another distinguishing factor is that Bil-Jac puts the customer first. While many companies give lip service to this goal, Bil-Jac practices what it preaches. Senior managers at Bil-Jac often answer the phones, so instead of reaching an automated attendant, customers with questions may find themselves talking with an officer of the company—often a Kelly himself. And at no time have customers been so grateful as during the 2007 pet-food recall.

"A lot of people suddenly thought, *Does the company making my dog food have control over all the ingredients in it?* Well, we do," says Jo Anne.

The phone rang off the hook for weeks. Jo Anne estimates they fielded four hundred calls a day. Callers were thrilled to reach a knowledgeable, friendly person who was happy to talk with them. They were even more delighted when they were told no Bil-Jac product was recalled or was likely ever to be recalled. They were relieved to learn that Bil-Jac does not use any gluten meals. Instead, all Bil-Jac dog foods contain only ingredients supplied by known, trusted U.S. suppliers,

April 2007

Petfood
WATT **Industry**

Bil-Jac Foods:
The art of processing

Bob Kelly, left, and his father Bill Kelly of Bil-Jac Foods, p. 20

Petfood Forum Europe guide

with each load inspected by Bil-Jac before being accepted for processing. This kind of personal assurance and quality control helps cement relationships and foster devoted followers.

"Answering the phones might not be the most efficient way of doing business, but the Kellys want to provide the personal touch, so that's how we do it," says Jo Anne.

Taking time to comfort customers, select top-quality ingredients, and build sales dog by dog is the Kelly way, and it works for them. Bil-Jac managers have learned to be patient. "In the seventeen years I've been with the company, the challenge has probably been in wanting to grow faster in some areas and do things a little bit more quickly than the way we do them now. But the Kellys want to make sure they don't grow just for the sake of growing. We have to make sure we have the right resources ready for customer follow-up and whatever else we need," Jo Anne says.

The result is a consistently exceptional product, batch after batch, and satisfied customers with confidence that the quality, safety, and nutrition of their dog's food will never be compromised. "It is a pleasure knowing we are putting the best product out there. I have believed it all along, but the recall reinforced it," Jo Anne affirms.

Chapter 13

DOING THE RIGHT THING

It is clear to everyone who knows Bill Kelly that he relishes being an entrepreneur. For more than sixty years he has devoted his life to developing the ideal dog food and building a strong company. But his family and community have always come first.

"He separated family from work. When he came home, he was *Dad*. He made a point that we should do the same thing, so today, work stays at work," says Jim.

"I can remember back in the early days, Dad always found time to go to the football, basketball, and Little League games we played in," adds Ray.

A sports fan and talented athlete himself, Bill used the principles of sportsmanship to raise his boys.

"Dad was a great coach, a life coach. He always encouraged us. He didn't yell and scream, and he wasn't a strict disciplinarian. He raised us by example, and you always knew where he stood," says Jim.

While there was no doubt that building a new business from scratch and raising three boys would have fulfilled most men, Bill found plenty of time to give back to his community.

One of the first community boards Bill was invited to join was that of Old Phoenix National Bank. It came about in a most unusual way.

In 1958, Bill came into the bank, sat down with a young loan officer named David B. Jones, and explained that his father had borrowed money from the bank around 1940 and had never repaid it. Bill said he wanted to pay back the entire

Harsh living conditions nearly destroyed Ch. Monomoy First von Faust ("Faust"), but Marianne Reder rescued him and restored his condition and self-esteem with tender loving care and Bil-Jac. He won his first championship only thirty days after he began showing.

LOVE AND BIL-JAC ....

When Marianne Reder first laid eyes on Faust, he was in pitiful condition. Although he had been bred by one of the country's leading Weimaraner kennels, he had not been treated well by one of his first owners.

"He was extremely thin, and his ears were hard, cracked, and bleeding. He had sores all over his body from being stropped, and he had been lying in urine so long that a sore on his chest was raw to the bone," Mrs. Reder remembers.

But what she saw under the ugliness took her breath away.

"He was beautiful—magnificent," she says, admitting it was love at first sight.

Faust was just the dog she wanted to breed to Ch. Stainless Steel Jelica Joy. Joy was Mrs. Reder's first Weimaraner and her first purebred show dog. Joy was as beautiful as she was smart, and she became the first dog to be certified as both American and Canadian TDX (Tracking Dog Excellent). Joy's ability to track human scent was so good that the American Kennel Club used her to develop their rules for TDX qualification.

Mrs. Reder packed up Faust in her powder blue Buick station wagon and drove him back to his owner and breeder, who cried when she saw his condition. The dog was so filthy that before he entered the house, Mrs. Reder bathed him with water from the garden hose and fragrant shampoo.

"He loved it so much that he rubbed his head on my jeans until I was soaked. He was a very proud animal and was embarrassed about his condition," Mrs. Reder says.

After a swim in the pool, a walk in the warm May afternoon, play time, and dinner, Faust had found a new lease on life. It was clear that he and Mrs. Reder had bonded. The breeder told her to take him home with her.

As soon as she arrived at Inomine Kennels in Cuyahoga Falls, Ohio, Mrs. Reder called her handler, Dick Becker, and they made a plan to recondition the seven-year-old dog.

"We soaked his ears in oil and doctored him. Of course, we fed him Bil-Jac. I was feeding it to Joy and had fed it to the pet dogs I had before her. In no time at all, he put on weight and his coat improved tremendously," Mrs. Reder says.

In only two months, Faust was ready to show. One month later, he had earned enough points to be a champion.

"He won nearly every time he went in the ring," says Mrs. Reder. "He was never what you would call a pretty dog, but he had attitude and an overriding presence. You couldn't take your eyes off him."

That same year, Ch. Monomoy First von Faust sired his first and only litter. Mrs. Reder sent the puppies to their carefully selected homes with a bag of Bil-Jac. She kept one puppy for herself, and eight generations later, she still insists that her puppies' new owners feed Bil-Jac. The lineage has produced more than fifty champions.

"I see Faust and Joy in every one of them," she says.

amount, stating that his father would have been bothered to know a debt had gone unpaid.

"His honesty and integrity astounded me," says Jones.

Jones never forgot Bill Kelly. About ten years later, after Jones had become president of Old Phoenix, he asked Bill to serve on the bank's board. Bill accepted and helped the bank set policies on how to deliver banking services, establish branches, hire officers, and establish what direction the bank's charitable giving would take.

"More than half our assets were located in the county, so we wanted to be part of the community. For many years, our objective was to provide the best, not necessarily the most profitable, services. Bill helped us immensely," says Jones.

• •

"I believe in foundations. They do such nice things for people," says Bill, who has established four charitable foundations.

In 1991, Bill established the first foundation at Medina General Hospital, on whose board he had served for thirty-eight years. According to Gary Hallman, the hospital's chief executive officer, Bill has the rare ability to look beyond the immediate and see what will be needed tomorrow.

"He saw that health care in Ohio was ready to break, and he predicted the hospital might not generate enough profit to fund capital projects. He wanted to do something about it, so he created a lifeblood channel to ensure the future of the hospital," says Hallman.

Bill made the first gift—$10,000—to the foundation he conceived and established. From this seed money, the foundation has grown to several million dollars in assets.

But Bill's generosity did not stop there. He also funds scholarships through the hospital that are awarded annually to two graduates of county schools who aspire to enter any medical or health-care field.

For his foresight and leadership, Bill was selected by the Center for Health Affairs to receive the Edward F. Meyers Outstanding Trustee Award in 2005. This prestigious award is presented annually to individuals who serve on the board of a Northeast Ohio hospital and who demonstrate excellence in leadership, are exceptionally

involved with the hospital they serve, and who serve as ambassadors in the community on behalf of the hospital.

Hallman feels blessed to know a man who gives so much and asks for so little in return. "Bill is a kind, generous human being and a private, gracious individual who takes little or no credit for what he does. Instead, he pats people on the back and gives them an 'atta boy.' I don't remember him saying a bad word about anybody or anything. He turns everything into a positive," says Hallman.

Bill's understanding of the value of his own employees also helped Medina General Hospital recognize the wisdom of supporting their own. At one time during the years Bill served as chairman of the hospital's Human Resources Committee, the board approved a 2 percent raise for the employees.

The next day, Bill dropped in to see Hallman. "Gary, your most important asset is your people. You have to treat them right. If you don't have good people, you won't be successful," he told the CEO. "I don't think 2 percent is good enough for the people you have. I think at least 3 percent is needed." The amount was changed.

"I thanked him for reminding us of the need to make things right," Hallman recalls.

• •

Twelve years ago, Bill joined the fledgling Highland High School Foundation for Educational Excellence. He recognized that the key to inspiring children to greater success was to excite them in middle school. In 2005 he and Ruth donated $110,000 to create a technical laboratory that makes computer learning fun. The class exposes children to sixteen different career areas and is mandatory for eighth graders.

"At that age, you can see they want to learn. By the time they get into high school, sometimes they get turned off. You have to reach them while they still have ambition," Bill explains.

He and Ruth also support two college scholarships, which are given to the most outstanding male and female students in the senior class. Recipients are chosen by the teachers.

Bill also gives a college scholarship at his former high school in Thompson, Ohio, and personally attends the ceremony.

The Kellys are church people, and Granger United Methodist has played a strong role in helping them feel blessed for the gifts they have received in life. As thanks, Bill helped establish a foundation that has grown over the years. Today, it provides college scholarships to church youth and supports mission programs and other activities in the church.

In recognition of Bill's generosity to the community where he and his employees live and work, the Medina Area Chamber of Commerce inducted Bill into their Hall of Fame in 2004.

Bill's philanthropy now extends beyond Northern Ohio to the East coast. In the last few years, Bil-Jac has become a major contributor to Atlantic General Hospital in Berlin, Maryland, where dry Bil-Jac is made.

• •

It was later in Bill's life that Hiram College rediscovered their former student, whose name had apparently been erased from the rolls when he did not graduate. Someone spotted Bill's name in a list of people who had entered Hiram as freshmen, recognized it, and invited him to attend his class's fiftieth reunion.

Bill was tickled pink, and so was Hiram. They quickly identified him as someone who represented the ideal Hiram student—an entrepreneur and pioneer who had a successful career—and soon invited him to join their Board of Visitors.

"He was the kind of person Hiram represented: the self-made person for whom Hiram made a difference," says Hiram's now-retired president Ben Oliver. "We felt it was important that our board composition reflect people who had real life experience in how Hiram transforms lives."

Unlike a policy-making board of trustees, Hiram's Board of Visitors brings together twenty astute business and civic leaders with different perspectives on the nature of education. Several times a year, they are invited to meet with the president to discuss an issue of concern to the college.

"He spoke seldom, but when he did, the board listened," Oliver remembers. "Some people comment on everything, but he was not a forward participator. The board understood why he was there, and he carried a real weight."

Hiram has a strong science department, and Bill's ability to talk to faculty about integrating science into economic development was invaluable to the college. "He had stayed current in protein amino acid assimilation in animals and could actually talk in a scientific way with young PhD professors, who were blown away by his knowledge and application to research and development. He taught us how to take pure knowledge and apply it to business," says Oliver.

Bill would have studied four years at Hiram and graduated if his family's circumstances had allowed. Fortunately, his former professor of biological sciences, J. Turner, had been more than willing to offer his expertise to help the young entrepreneur find the optimal combination of amino acids for canine nutrition. In recognition of Turner, Bill established the William H. and Ruth Kelly Endowed Scholarship, which is given to a deserving entering or upper-class student with an interest or major in science, preferably biological sciences or chemistry.

Bill continues to influence generations of Hiram College graduates who share his entrepreneurial spirit: He convinced Hiram that they needed to teach entrepreneurship. "I pushed them to teach it, because you can go all over the world, and you don't have the opportunities, the work ethic, and the laws that we have in this country. You have to live in an environment that promotes it, fosters it, and makes it possible," says Bill.

In 1993, Hiram College awarded Bill their highest honor—membership in the Garfield Society. The Garfield Society had been established by Hiram's Board of Trustees in 1972 to honor outstanding civic and business leaders, Hiram College trustees, and Hiram faculty who have earned the rank of full professor. The Garfield Society is named for the twentieth president of the United States, James A. Garfield, a former Hiram student, faculty member, and president.

. . . .

Because Bill led by example, his sons saw the benefits of charitable work and followed in his footsteps. "We became involved because it was clear Dad enjoyed it. It wasn't like a chore or a duty," says Jim.

Bob served on the Medina County Board of Education for sixteen years and has served on the Highland Board of Education since 1998. He also serves on the Board of Advisors of First Merit Bank, which purchased Old Phoenix. But the thrust of Bob's charitable service developed in an unexpected way and with a more personal touch. Bob and his

wife, Becky, have brought twelve children into their family.

It started when his wife's sister separated from her husband, and Bob and Becky took over raising her third-grade son, Andrew. The boy settled in, and the arrangement became permanent.

Drew went on to graduate from Ohio University, Bob's alma mater, marry, and have two beautiful children.

When Drew was in high school, Bob and Becky were asked to take in a French foreign exchange student whose destination family had a medical emergency and was unable to accommodate her at the last minute. The arrangement worked so well that the sponsors continued to ask the Kellys to host foreign students. Over the years, the family hosted two girls from France and boys from Mexico, Germany, and Spain.

The German boy was six feet nine. He started playing basketball and other sports at Highland High School, and that year, the school won the Suburban League Championship. Eventually, the boy received a full basketball scholarship to Penn State, and now plays professionally in Europe.

His success started a trend. "We found out there were groups that help students who have no money to come over here, so we got involved

in doing that," says Bob. A number of them were athletes with the ability to obtain college sports scholarships. The first two were from Lithuania. One attended the University of Arizona, was drafted by the San Antonio Spurs, and today earns millions a year playing professionally in Europe. The other attended the University of Pittsburgh and also plays professionally in Europe.

The following year, two basketball players from Mali ended up in the Kelly household. One had been orphaned; the other's parents were desperately poor. Bob and Becky tried to adopt both boys, but the boys were considered too old. Nevertheless, Bob and Becky consider them their sons. Both attended college on scholarships, obtained professional positions, and are currently in the process of becoming naturalized citizens. The Kellys have taken in other children from Mali and Brazil in the past nine years.

"We have a huge international family. They were God's gift to us, because we couldn't have kids," says Bob, who admits they talk to all twelve children regularly. "They are still such a huge part of our family. It's where we choose to put our resources and focus, and it's rewarding. We got that from Dad and Mom," he says.

• • • • • • • • • • • • • • • • • • •

In the late 1970s, Julie Nivins began working in the Bil-Jac offices. Julie spotted the growing sales trend in the grocery segment and took it upon herself to compile the sales statistics for those stores. The stats helped Ray's work in the emerging grocery sales division.

Ray and Julie celebrated their twenty-fifth wedding anniversary in 2008. Although Julie no longer works at Bil-Jac, her influence is felt every day in the beautiful interior design of the new corporate offices.

Ray and Julie have two children of their own. Michael is studying business and plans on a career at Bil-Jac. Erin, the younger child, is crazy about horses and wants to be a horse trainer when she gets older. She's also crazy about her grandfather. "He's awesome," she says without reservation. "Whenever you walk into a room, he gives you a big hug."

Erin's competitive spirit and love for horses came together in the summer of 2007, when she placed first in her first horse show.

As much as Erin loves horses, she is equally crazy about her dog, a Boxer named Casey. She also knows her grandfather is a magnet, not only for people, but also for dogs. "When Casey walks into a room, the first person she'll go to is my grandpa," says Erin. "He loves it."

• •

Jim got married in the early nineties and welcomed three beautiful stepdaughters into his life. They were fifteen, twelve, and ten. He and his wife, Gail, have a son, Ben. Gail enjoys one-on-one time with Bill, just listening to him talk about life. "I have never heard anyone use the word 'special' more than Bill does," she says. "He looks at so many aspects of his life as being special. Just being around him makes you feel that way, too!"

Their oldest daughter, Jennifer, started doing in-store demonstrations for Bil-Jac as a senior in high school. During her four years at Wittenberg University, she continued to do demos in Springfield, Ohio, and other locations. After receiving her graduate degree in behavioral counseling at Wright State University, Jennifer moved to Houston to take over a Bil-Jac sales territory. A couple of years later, she decided to pursue her degreed field and is now working with high-risk inner-city children in Dayton. However, she does admit to missing the customer relationships she built while working for Bil-Jac.

Jennifer's younger sisters, Elizabeth and Katie, both had after-school and summer jobs in the Bil-Jac offices. Elizabeth is a new wife and mother and is working with young children. Katie is attending beauty school. Ben, who has not even reached his preteen years, has said for years that he wants to be a scientist. That puts a big smile on his grandpa's face. Ben has already helped conduct some feeding tests with his own dogs, Daisy, a loving Golden Retriever, and Kal, an athletic Chesapeake Bay Retriever.

Like his father and brothers, Jim finds time to enrich the lives of children in his community. His first experience was serving on the Board of Directors of Community United Head Start, a Cleveland agency that provides families with quality education, literacy programs, social services, and related support.

Jim currently serves on the board of the Highland Foundation, where he has helped fund work internships for the local high school, matching kids' interests with the needs of local businesses. "We need to get our kids integrated into our community to keep them here. They need to see there is potential," he says. "We have found that when you line up the right kid with the right job, it lights a fire in them. The employers are thrilled, and they tell us the kids always exceed their expectations. It's a win-win situation."

Up to twenty students a year from two Medina County high schools have been placed with employers in a wide range of businesses, and Jim is working with the Economic Development Board and other civic organizations to expand the number of participating employers and high schools. "Our blueprint has been so successful that we are trying to implement the program in all seven county school districts," he says.

Although the project is time-consuming, Jim has recently become involved in another organization that promises to be worth every minute he can spare for it. It's W.A.G.S. 4 Kids, an organization that trains assistance dogs and provides them to disabled children at no cost.

"It's a phenomenal help to them," Jim says—and a fitting match for a man who loves both children and dogs.

Chapter 14 ....

BIL-JAC LOOKS TO THE FUTURE

The Kellys have had plenty of opportunities to sell their company, but they are not interested. They are sure any company willing to pay billions of dollars for the name would compromise the quality of their products by substituting less expensive, less nutritious ingredients. For a family dedicated to perfecting a formula, this is unthinkable.

"Bill does it for quality, not money, and Bob is cut out of the same cloth," says Charles ("Chuck") Emrick, Bil-Jac Foods' former attorney. For this reason, Bill turned to Emrick to create a succession plan that would ensure the company stays in the Kelly family, even in the unlikely chance that one of the Kelly boys decides to call it quits.

Because the company is privately held, Bil-Jac has no board of trustees. Instead, the Kellys established an advisory board to help them grow the business in a methodical way. As "outsiders" with fresh perspective, advisory board members provide valuable input on a number of issues ranging from expansion to sales to the creation of new products.

"They are a company that stays true to their culture, which is making the best product available. Their strength is their understanding of biochemistry," says advisory board member Rob McCreary. "We are encouraging them to be more market-driven."

In addition to the original frozen Bil-Jac, the company makes several types of dry Bil-Jac for dogs of various ages and weights, as well as several different dog and cat treats. Cat treats are made at the same plant where dog treats are

Gary Gero with the Neapolitan Mastiff in England on the set of Harry Potter and the Half-Blood Prince. *One of the busiest and most respected trainers of animals for movies and television, Gero uses Bil-Jac dog food to feed his dogs and Bil-Jac liver treats to reward his dogs.*

BIL-JAC GOES TO HOLLYWOOD

One of America's busiest and most respected animal trainers, Gary Gero has been teaching animals and birds to perform in movies, television, and commercials for more than forty years. This month, Gero is on the set of *Harry Potter and the Half-Blood Prince* with an enormous Neapolitan Mastiff, who plays Fang. For one scene, he has taught Fang to accompany the character Hagrid out of a burning house, down the stairs, and across a field before stopping and looking up at his master. The dog's reward? A tasty Bil-Jac liver treat.

"We use the treats as positive reinforcement. The animals love them, and it keeps them motivated," Gero explains.

Rather than training the animals by using the treats as bait, he teaches them to respond to hand signals and voice commands. When they perform a behavior correctly, he offers praise and a Bil-Jac liver treat.

Gero has been using Bil-Jac food and treats exclusively for so long, he can't remember when he first started using the brand. He could use any brand he wanted, but he remains loyal to Bil-Jac.

"We go through cases and cases of treats in the training process, so I have to use the best and healthiest treats available. Bil-Jac is quality. Just look at my dogs. They have perfect coats and are healthy and full of energy," he says.

The list of famous Bil-Jac dogs trained by Gero's company, Birds and Animals Unlimited, includes Moose, who played Eddie on *Frasier*; the Golden Retriever and Bulldog puppy in *Homeward Bound: The Incredible Journey*; all 101 Dalmatians; Marley in *Marley & Me*; the Huskies in *Eight Below*; and the Chihuahuas in *Beverly Hills Chihuahua*.

According to Gero, many animals besides dogs like Bil-Jac dog food, too. He feeds it to ravens, crows, raccoons, skunks, foxes, and cats. The next time you see the 2006 version of the movie *Lassie*, watch for the foxes running from a pack of foxhounds. Gero trained the year-old animals to navigate various natural obstacle courses, stopping periodically in front of the camera on a small mark. The intelligent animals were able to learn their patterns in about ten minutes and were rewarded with Bil-Jac liver treats.

"Foxes aren't like dogs, but they are as smart as dogs, and they love Bil-Jac, too," says Gero.

made and continue to be bestsellers. The line is continually expanding.

"They are so good at creating good products that we would like to see them extend that knowledge to the treats business. The line is not as extensive as it could be, and it's a huge opportunity," says McCreary. "There are endless possibilities to expand the company, but they want to get things perfect. And part of what comes with a family business is that you control the company. You can do what you want," he adds.

One advisory board member with experience and expertise particularly valuable to the Kellys is Richard Osborne, professor of the practice of management policy at Case Western Reserve University's Weatherhead School of Management. Osborne started a career in banking but left at a young age to run a family-owned company. He is intimately familiar with the challenges of a private business and has a great deal of respect for how Bil-Jac is run.

"I have served on twenty-five boards and helped organize a dozen advisory boards, and this is a gem of a company in terms of their business model, products, and management philosophy. You don't run into companies like this very often," Osborne says. "The Kellys are an admirable family. You have to respect the way their values permeate the business, and the fact that these values are acted upon and not merely stated in a poster or brochure. They are a values-driven business succeeding in a land of giants."

Osborne calls the Kellys "the all-time straight arrows," who put integrity ahead of profits. "No matter the competition, no one ever attempts to compromise the integrity of the product to increase profit. The animals' health has always come first," says Osborne.

The uniqueness of this product-driven, uncompromising approach in the face of cutthroat competition made Bil-Jac an ideal case study for MBA students in Osborne's program. For several years, the Kellys spoke to his class, which studied the company and analyzed its business practices.

"It was a fun company to study due to the nature of their product," Osborne says. "In addition, they are such a lovely family. The boys are deeply affectionate and respectful of their father. They know how to treat people and animals, and the company is imbued by the family's attitude," he says. "It's a chance to show what a values-driven business looks like and to communicate that good guys can finish first."

Bill and Ruth Kelly

One fact about Bil-Jac that frustrates advisory board members is that this great company's "amazing" product is still unknown to many pet owners. This is in no small part due to the influence of their conglomerate competitors' multimillion-dollar advertising budgets. However, word of mouth by satisfied customers continues to spread the good word and influence new customers to try Bil-Jac.

Osborne is excited about the opportunities for growth in international markets, as ventures in Japan, Malaysia, Korea, Israel, Chile, Canada, and other countries are growing the sale of Bil-Jac dog food and treats.

"In the long-term, international opportunities may change the business in ways that selling abroad changes every business, but Bil-Jac's uncompromising passion for quality will never change," says Osborne.

• •

One person preparing to tackle these challenges is Ray Kelly's son, Michael, the most likely Kelly to carry on the legacy. A serious young man and excellent student, Michael entered college in the fall of 2007 with the aim of attaining a business degree. After graduation, he plans to get an MBA. This, he feels, will enable him to enter the family business armed with the knowledge he needs to increase Bil-Jac's market share. "It's a three-generation thing, and I'd hate to lose that. I really enjoy the family setting," he says.

Like his father and uncles, Michael worked nights and weekends at Bil-Jac, starting at the bottom with cleaning, hosing, and packing. He quickly understood the value of his experience.

"You have to learn everything before you have respect for it. I have so much respect for the factory guys that do the same thing every day. It's just hard work," Michael admits.

Michael talks to his grandfather at least twice a week, tapping Bill's source of business knowledge and investments.

"I think my grandpa is very charismatic. There's so much he's done, and I still don't know everything. Every time I go to his office, he tells me a story that I haven't heard before. It's mind-boggling how much he accomplished, even when he was my age," says Michael.

Michael agrees that the future of Bil-Jac will continue to be found in international markets, and to this end, he is focusing on international business. "I like the challenge, I guess," he says.

China has rapidly growing upper and middle classes that have embraced small dogs as status symbols. But China, Korea, and other Asian countries do not have strong laws that protect patents, leaving Bil-Jac's formula and name open to potential theft. Michael is unfazed by such obstacles. "I mean, that's why you go to college, to figure out what you can do about situations like this," he says.

Michael is also preparing to handle domestic issues, which he views with fresh perspective. "I'd like to see more in the marketing field than we have right now, because we do a lot by word of mouth. I think we should be doing more demos. I just like customer interaction with the product, the one-on-one," he says.

Jim, Ray, Bill, and Bob Kelly in 2007. Like their 1951 delivery truck, their company was built on old-fashioned values that have stood the test of time.

Michael loves to demonstrate what happens when dry Bil-Jac and another popular brand of dry dog food—any brand—are put in separate cups of water. The dry Bil-Jac dissolves, while the other food absorbs water and puffs up like popcorn.

"You say to the customer, 'Look at this. Your dog is not getting anything but puffed up pieces of nothing. With Bil-Jac, you get all the nutrients.' This is so much more effective than throwing an

Bil-Jac is a rarity—a successful family business in an industry dominated by corporate giants. The future of Bil-Jac lies with Michael Kelly (fourth from left), who looks forward to taking Bil-Jac into new markets. He is shown with three generations of family: (from left to right) Ray, Julie, Erin, and Michael Kelly; Ruth and Bill Kelly; Becky and Bob Kelly; Ben, Gail, and Jim Kelly. The dog on Bill's lap is Moose, the Jack Russell Terrier that played Eddie in the hit television series, Frasier. Moose was a Bil-Jac dog.

ad on TV or giving someone a coupon you don't know if they will redeem," he says.

Because Bil-Jac's products were not involved in the 2007 pet-food recall, sales of Bil-Jac increased dramatically following the recall. Michael clearly understands how taking the extra steps to ensure quality control reinforced their reputation.

"There's no way that the recall could ever have happened to our products," he says. "We screen everything that goes into Bil-Jac."

Like his father and uncles, Michael admires what his grandfather was able to accomplish through hard work and shows respect for the fruits of those labors.

"I am grateful for what I have. I have a really nice life because of how much he sacrificed when he was younger. We are a humble family. We don't really flaunt. We do what we have to do and don't make a big fuss out of it," says Michael.

"I'm blessed, and it's mostly because of what the company has done," he continues. "It was by no means easy work. Grandpa started the company on thirty bucks and worked twelve- and fourteen-hour days. He's over ninety years old and is still coming to the office and giving his sons insightful pointers. He still has a fire under him. I hope there's still a fire under me when I'm ninety years old," says Michael.

• •

In the future, Bil-Jac management will change. The market is already changing, and the way Bil-Jac approaches sales and distribution may have to change in order to maintain or increase market share. But one thing dog owners can count on is that Bil-Jac itself will never change, unless it's for the better. That's because Bill Kelly's vision remains solidly in place. From day one, he understood the importance American families place on their beloved pets. And just like their customers, members of the Bil-Jac family of employees go home every night to a joyous reunion with their dogs. That's what drives them to make the tastiest, most nutritious dog food in the world.

Making pet food is Bil-Jac's only business. However, this American success story is so much more than a business: for Bill Kelly and his family, Bil-Jac is their life's work and passion. An idea that started over sixty years ago "because dogs deserved better" has become the industry standard and a serious competitor to foods produced by corporations many times Bil-Jac's size. But the true testament to Bil-Jac's phenomenal popularity rests not in sales figures, nor in name recognition, but rather in the millions and millions of healthy, beautiful dogs that have lived long and happy lives on Bil-Jac.